THE LONG RIDERS

An Anthology of Amazing Equestrian Travel Stories

Volume One

Edited by
CuChullaine' O'Reilly

ISBN: 1-59048-138-0

The Long Riders' Guild Press 2004

Cover illustration: Long Rider George Beck on his
Morab gelding, Pinto, taken at Atlanta, Georgia,
June 5th 1913.

www.horsetravelbooks.com

DEDICATION

This book is dedicated to the memory of the Overland Westerners, George Beck, Charles Beck, Jay Ransom and Raymond Rayne, who hold the unofficial record for the longest continual equestrian journey of the 20th century.

Setting off from the tiny village of Shelton, Washington on May 1, 1912 the four men rode through all forty eight states, thereby visiting each capitol and meeting their governors. During their non-stop three year journey the Overland Westerners traveled 20,352 miles in the saddle. Only one horse, a hardy Morab gelding named Pinto, managed to complete the entire trip.

Expecting fanfare upon the completion of their historic pilgrimage in San Francisco, California, on June 1, 1915, they were bitterly disappointed to discover an apathetic public more interested in the new fangled horseless carriage. Their remarkable equestrian achievement has been overlooked for nearly a century.

When recently informed of this oversight, the Guinness Book of World Records expressed the opinion that the record-setting equestrian accomplishment was of no historical significance.

How wrong they were !

Rest easy, Long Riders.

www.horsetravelbooks.com

There is no solace on earth for us - for such as we, who
search for the hidden beauties that eye may never see.
Only the road and the dawn, the sun, the wind, and the rain,
and the watch - fire under the stars, and sleep, and the road again.

John Masefield

Contents

Page

Introduction 9
Chapter 1 – Mexican Bandits, by Joseph Carl Goodwin.............................11
Chapter 2 – Last of the Saddle Tramps, by Messanie Wilkins....................17
Chapter 3 – Dead Horse Pass, by Wilfred Skrede...22
Chapter 4 – Ride a White Horse, by William Holt.......................................28
Chapter 5 – An Instinctive Passion, by Charles Darwin 35
Chapter 6 – A Journey to Simplify Life, by D. C. Vision............................42
Chapter 7 – Through Russia on a Mustang, by Thomas Stevens.................47
Chapter 8 – Jungle Assault, by Sharon Muir Watson 53
Chapter 9 – Blizzard and Blindness, by Donald Brown..............................60
Chapter 10 – Forgotten Heroes, by Darcy Morger-Grovenstein.....................65
Chapter 11 – Winter Sketches from the Saddle, by John Codman.................72
Chapter 12 – Through Persia on a Sidesaddle, by Ella Sykes.........................78
Chapter 13 – California Coast Trails, by J. Smeaton Chase...........................85
Chapter 14 – Eastward Ho! Into Asia, by Anna Louise Strong 89
Chapter 15 – My Kingdom for a Horse, by Margaret Leigh............................96
Chapter 16 – My Horse, my Husband, and I, by Ria Bosman Naysmith......103
Chapter 17 – Riding from the Flames, by Lady Florence Dixie 115
Chapter 18 – Khyber Knights, by CuChullaine O'Reilly 119
Chapter 19 – Vagabond, by Jeremy James..130
Chapter 20 – Saddlebags for Suitcases, by Mary Bosanquet 134

Epilogue: Equestrian Argonauts, The Story of The Long Riders'
Guild, by Darcy Morger-Grovenstein 140

Introduction

History, they say, is the best teacher. The tragedy is that we have discovered too late that many painful lessons of the past regarding equestrian travel have either been lost or forgotten. The collective equestrian knowledge passed on by generations of nomads has vanished. As 21st century horsemen and women we have access to amazing equine medical technology, space age tack and global positioning satellites that can track our every move. It has never been safer to venture away from home on your horse.

Yet too often those few who ride out into the unknown do so with little or no knowledge of the rigors and dangers required by long distance equestrian exploration and travel. They set off in search of Aimee Tschiffely's dream and end up painfully reinventing the equestrian wheel due to a pathetic lack of hands-on knowledge. Hopefully, the reader will find lodged in these stories the living lessons previous travelers saw fit to share.

Plus, as one who has ridden the hard road, I know first hand that an equestrian traveler is forever receiving help, food, shelter and sympathy. This book is an attempt to repay in some small portion the wealth of kindness I have received from strangers during my various travels.

In closing, I know it is vain to reason with some people. One might as well argue with a teapot as try to explain the mysteries and beauties of equestrian travel to my skeptics.

To those who scoff at this antiquated mode of travel I so deeply admire I say only this, happiness comes to those who boldly participate in the adventure of life. The critics speak of hardship and I reply the real hardship is to be a dull fool. Too many people are content to ride at anchor in the safe harbor of their regulated lives, never traveling, scudding from one safe spot to another as a succession of nameless, muddy days fill out their lives.

This book is not for them. It is aimed at those few rugged individualists for whom the essence of life is the distant horizon.

For on journeys such as these, the equestrian traveler learns one of the lost nomad secrets; we who travel do not possess our horses, they possess us, body and soul. Together we have passed through an invisible curtain, entering an uncharted, new world where only the journey is constant. Such a rider and such a horse no longer belong to warm rooms, regular meals, and the comfort of certain safety. We are part of rivers and forests, wild weather and wilder mountains. We no longer travel to arrive, for horse and rider have grown content to journey on steadily, suspended in time as we venture from one unknown to another.

Equestrian travel is full of such vital, urgent days and this lasting, simple truth.

You who have never traveled far on horseback have never tasted the salt of life!

Chapter 1
Mexican Bandits
by
Joseph Carl Goodwin

At first glance one may wonder how qualified were the two young men who set off from a Texas border town bound for Mexico City in 1931. The author, a Yankee with an itchy foot, was hungry for a taste of peril. His companion, Robert Horiguichi, was the sophisticated son of an imperial Japanese diplomat.

To say the two mismatched, would-be equestrian explorers were unprepared for the deserts, quicksand and brigands they encountered in the Mexican wilderness would be a mild understatement. Luckily before leaving the Lone Star state they had procured what they thought were the necessities of equestrian travel, including a canteen, an old pistol and a typewriter to chronicle their adventures. Along with their mustangs, Pistole and Negra, the amateur adventurers set out to prove that the dangers of the road were as welcome – and far more satisfying – than the pleasures.

Mexican bandits seem to function in epidemics. For weeks, months, even years, nothing is heard of them. Then, one day, comes report of a train robbed near Pachucha or Monterey. The next day a village is sacked down in Sonora, or a haciendado and his retainers are slain in the state of San Luis Potosi. From these isolated cases the contagion spreads and robbery, arson, murder and rapine ride on the hoofs of bandits' ponies.

Since the first days after the trail at Villa Acuna, Bob and I had heard only scattered warnings against brigands. And during the entire thirty-nine days it took our horses to plod the long route to Jilotepec, we had seen no one who threatened us any harm. We had come to feel that the whole thing was a popular myth, that there were no bandits in any of the towns through which we passed.

In fact, we decided, if there were any outlaws in any part of the republic, they were probably tame compared to the "tough guys" in the United States. The warnings, we believed, came from persons who only feared the next village contained vicious individuals because the next village was too far away to be familiar, and unfamiliar things are fearful to primitive minds.

Rumors of bandit activities had begun again at San Luis Potosi. There was labor trouble on the railroad in the north. A train was derailed. Nothing had been taken and no one was injured but shots had been fired at fleeing horsemen.

News travels slowly in the ranch country. At Santa Domingo, Arroyo Zarco and Chichemecas there was no word of "los banditos." But the owner of Santo Domingo displayed a muscular forearm which had been torn by a bullet in a raid a few years earlier and the stucco walls of Chichemecas were as badly pitted as a pock-marked face.

At San Juan del Rio and at San Luis de la Paz, tidings had seeped in of sanguinary raids on villages and haciendas in the mountains of eastern Hidalgo. In a cafe at Jilotepec, we heard that one band of brigands had been so brazen as to venture into the very heart of Mexico, practically under the noses of the soldados posted in all the towns surrounding the Federal District and the capital.

Myth or no myth, the morning Bob and I left Jilotepec, we voiced our thanks for having been spared an encounter with the lawless. With few exceptions, our associations in the republic had been only the most pleasant. Now, with the ancient stronghold of the Aztec only seventy kilometers to the south, we felt that danger was past. Already we had run the gauntlet of the wild country.

At any rate, we agreed, we appeared so much like poor, travel-weary natives that robbers would consider us unworthy of their efforts. Bob, with his combined European and Oriental inheritances, often had been mistaken for a Mexican and I, being a descendent of the "Black Irish" might pass as a native of Mexico if I were not too closely observed.

The slow trip across the desert and mountain, under a tropical sun, had resulted in our being burned to a similar shade of mahogany brown. Our clothing, blue denim and khaki, boots and straw sombreros – was bleached in spots, muddy in spots and ragged in entirety. Our horses, which had borne us over a thousand miles of the roughest country in the Mexican republic, were too emaciated and bedraggled to attract the covetous. Our general appearance had been planned from the very start as a measure of protection should we wander into the ken of outlaws.

Nevertheless, one of us always carried the pistol given us by Señor Trevino, in a side pocket of his trousers during the day and under his head at night.

We left Jilotepec on the morning of August fourth, the wet season was entering its final and most active half. The river, where we crossed over an ancient bridge at the pueblo's end, was a sucking, swirling flood as thick as flowing lava.

The sheets of water through which we had trudged the day before had ceased. But the atmosphere was so saturated it seemed to sweat large, cold drops that somehow found a way under the rubber cape draped from my throat, down over the saddle and below my boot tops. Every plant and native hut along the trail appeared to shrug its shoulders and hump over to keep out the dampness.

A road had been started toward the city of Mexico, and Bob and I, heads ducked against the clammy breezes, turned our horses into the yellow quagmire. For hours we trudged along, climbing over high, muddy, ridges, sliding down into wide, muddy valleys, skirting streams that had left their banks – pushing on in hopes of reaching the capital by night.

About the middle of the day we entered a half-flooded valley north of Tepotzotlan. We were damp, hungry and generally uncomfortable. The horses dragged along through soft, black mud that reached to their knees. Before us in the distance was the bare, earthen-stepped hillside that climbs up to Tepotzotlan and Cuautitlan. Behind us, at a greater distance, were the green and slate-colored slopes over which our trail had led from Jilotepec.

The entire valley, as far as we could see through the perspiring atmosphere, was uninhabited and deserted.

But suddenly, there sounded the echo of a shout and a faraway flutter of laughter. A long survey of the road ahead revealed a moving patch of color, which in due time, spread to take the form of horsemen coming toward us. Soon we knew there were four of them and they all carried rifles. Even before we were able to discern their faces under the drooping brims of their sombreros, we had decided they were drunk.

We looked for a way to go around them. But the heavy rains had flooded the flat lands on either side of us. Only the newly built road toward the capital was above water and it was knee deep in mud.

"I don't like the look of this," said Bob and I agreed. "We had better meet them as calmly as possible though – just as if we were old pals. Maybe they will think we are not worth stopping – or maybe they are only going hunting," he said and laughed nervously. I, too, was making a pretense of taking the entire matter lightly.

I drew the pistol from my pocket and gripped it firmly, concealed by the folds of my rain cape. The four men had drawn nearer. Proximity revealed they also carried side arms. When we were within hailing distance they slowed their horses to a walk. They no longer talked or laughed. We continued at a steady pace, almost fearlessly.

Then they stopped.

Three of them were facing us and the fourth turned his horse crossways in the road. A guitar was suspended about this neck, – above a cartridge belt. He ran his fingers over the strings with studied carelessness.

"Keep going," mumbled Bob, in English. "They're just drunk. They'll probably only ask for a match or a cigarette."

His attempt to maintain his Oriental stoicism failed. There was a new huskiness in his voice.

"Maybe so," I answered. "But you be ready to kick that plug of yours if have to make a run for it. In the meantime, start some of the diplomatic chatter of yours. This is one time it ought to be appreciated."

Time and time again, Bob's perfect command of Spanish had convinced persons, already deceived by his appearance, that he was a native Mexican. In addition to a faultless use of English, he conversed freely in his mother's native French, his father's Japanese, as well as German, Portuguese and Spanish. His linguistic ear was so delicately tuned that, as we passed through different states, he was able to alter his own expression and accent to conform to local dialects.

"Buenas tardes, señores," Bob addressed the waiting men.

We were less than twenty steps away from them.

"Hay mucha agua, no?"

There was a mumbled "buenas tardes" from one of the four. Their hands hovered near their belts. The carbines still were slung over their shoulders. We stopped immediately before them when the one who stood across our path gave no indication of moving to let us pass. Bob talked on, voicing various strained pleasantries concerning the weather.

Three of the men began to edge their horses forward, two on one side of us, one on the other.

I turned in the saddle to face the man behind Bob. My friend caught the movement and slid around to watch the man on my right flank. The third man dropped from his horse into the mud of the road.

My horse, Pistole, became nervous and started twitching. Even Bob's mount, the placid Negra, had his ears up and was chewing at the bit.

The Mexican standing in the road asked for a match and stepped toward me. At that moment I caught a glimpse of steel in the hand of the brigand behind Bob.

"Kick out your horse," I screamed, spurring Pistole with both heels and firing the automatic twice in the face of the man who asked for a match.

Bob, with all his seeming lack of suspicion, was completely alert and Negra leaped forward with the same movement that carried Pistole toward the man blocking our path.

Again I fired twice, this time at the human obstacle before us. His horse reared, fanning with fore feet as Bob and I scurried past with heads low. I glanced up, still kicking Pistole and saw the bandit slash at Bob with a machete. Evidently my last two shots had gone wild. Bob meanwhile was cursing in French.

In that tense moment it seemed ludicrous, – my Japanese companion cursing Mexican bandits in French – and I laughed, slightly hysterical, as we ran from the bullets that now began snapping at us and biting into the mud at the horses feet.

The frightened animals plunged wildly through the deep mire. We were lying flat along their necks, spurring them at every jump. Long after we were safe, we continued running.

When our assailants had stopped their wildly inaccurate firing and our hearts had ceased pumping like Gatling guns, we stopped to look back. Three of the bandits were standing in the road, looking down at a fourth who was lying in the mud. We did not go back to see if he was wounded or dead. We hurried on, forded a swollen stream and climbed across a hill of mud to reach Tepotzotlan, passing through fertile fields and orchards, peering back like pursued criminals and not pausing until we reached the village of Cuautitlan.

When we got there, Bob slipped into a drogueria[1] and bought a dressing for a machete wound in his arm and a salve for the bullet burn running across my back. After we were hidden safely, with our horses in the back of a public stable and exchanging first aid treatment, Bob asked, "When did that shot graze you?"

"I don't know. I didn't feel it at the time. But it sure burns like hell now. When you get yours?"

"I didn't know I had it until after we got away. That bruiser with the machete must have come closer than I thought," he said. "And look at my raincoat. The entire arm is ruined !"

I held up my cape for inspection. There were two neat round holes high up on the back.

"Great, this is the rainy season," I sputtered, but my anger lacked conviction. "Why those dirty, louse-ridden brigands. Let's go back and clean out the whole blasted outfit."

But despite our boasting, our laughter sputtered nervously like drops of rain in an open fire.

This is an excerpt from "Through Mexico on Horseback" by Joseph Carl Goodwin.

---

[1] Editor's note: Pharmacy.

Joseph Carl Goodwin with Pistole and Robert Horiguichi with Negra.

Chapter 2
Last of the Saddle Tramps
by
Messanie Wilkins

The world of equestrian travel has historically contained an exciting mixture of unique men and women. Some are adventurers seeking danger from the back of their horse. Others are travelers discovering the beauties of the countryside they slowly ride through. A few are exploring inner truths while cantering across desolate parts of the planet. Then there is Messanie Wilkins. She was acting on orders from the Lord!

In 1954, at the age of 63, Wilkins had plenty to worry about. A spinster, she had lost all the members of her family, the ancestral Maine farm and finally her health. After severe pneumonia nearly killed her, a doctor told her she had two years to live, provided she spent them quietly.

With no family ties, no money and no future in Maine, Wilkins decided to take a daring step. Recalling that her mother had always had a "hankerin'" to see California, the homespun lady-farmer turned equestrian explorer. Using the money she made from selling homemade pickles, she purchased Tarzan, a tired summer camp horse. Then, with an old coat on her back, a gas station map of America in hand and $32 dollars in her pocket, Wilkins decided she was ready to ride away from everything she had ever known, even if it killed her. At the last moment Messanie felt she needed confirmation that the Lord was in favor of her rash enterprise.

She flipped a nickel, heads to go-tails to stay. It came up heads three times running. So Messanie Mabel Wilkins, a humble American heroine, rode away on a 7,000 mile journey, bound for adventure and the Pacific Ocean.

A town called Media, Pennsylvania was our next stop. There was a nice-looking inn there, and while I pondered whether we could afford it, the innkeeper came outside and extended an invitation. He'd just bought a horse, so he had the place and the feed for Tarzan.

The Lions Club was dining at the inn that night, and the chairman asked me to be the club's special guest. I told him I was weary. Then when he told me they were having steak, I changed my mind about being weary.

After supper, the Lions took care of old and new business. The chairman introduced me and asked me to say a few words. I'd never made a speech in my life, but the gentlemen asked questions and got me started, and after that it was easy. I told then about how I'd bought Tarzan with pickle money, and about my coin-tossing agreement with the Lord, and about my life in Maine. They laughed and applauded every time I told them something new, and finally I was laughing so hard I couldn't continue.

Up until this experience, I'd always thought the life I'd lived was a pretty hard one. I'd never seen much fun in it, but here I was in Media, Pennsylvania laughing about it. There was a lesson in it for me. I didn't know what it was. Uncle Waldo would have known, but he wasn't alive to tell me. All I knew was what I felt. When I climbed into bed that night, I felt happier than ever before.

Chadd's Ford was only ten miles from Media, but they were the longest ten miles in Pennsylvania. A man at the inn had told me about a dirt road shortcut. We found the road without any trouble, but it took us two days to find Chadd's Ford.

The town had a big inn, too, although it seemed more like a hotel. Chadd's Ford Inn, it was called, and Mr. Flaherty, the manager, invited us to stay there. Tarzan was put up in a stable that hadn't housed a horse in years.

After I signed the register, they showed me an older one. The last signature in it belonged to the man who rode horseback from California to the New York World Fair in 1939. He still had some distance to go and had already worn out seven horses. That made me think Tarzan was a miracle horse. He looked fitter than when we'd started.

When I went out to saddle Tarzan the next morning, I found that he had company. A man was sitting there on a box and making a drawing of my horse.

"I hope you don't mind," he said. "I heard you were here and I wanted to make a head sketch of Tarzan. I'm almost finished." When I didn't say anything, he added, "my name is Andrew Wyeth. Mr. Flaherty knows me."

I looked over his shoulder as he worked, and I liked what I saw. I could tell it was Tarzan, and not just any horse. "You're pretty good," I told him.[2]

"Thank you," he said. He added a few lines to the drawing then stood up and thanked me again. I had to walk about ten feet to get the saddle, and when I turned around Mr. Wyeth was gone.

When we left the inn a half hour later, a light, wet snow was falling. It was slippery underfoot, and I made sure Tarzan kept to a slow walk. Cars made a swishing sound on the wet road as they passed us, and that always made Tarzan want to dance a bit.

---

[2] Editor's note: Messanie obviously didn't realize that Andrew Wyeth was (and still is) one of the most famous living artists in the United States!

The road brought us up a slight grade to the bridge that crossed Brandywine, which is a river or a creek, depending upon the person talking about it. It was a two-lane paved road, with wire cables strung along the sides to keep cars from rolling over embankments. I had a fine view of Brandywine Battlefield Park where one of the great battles of Revolutionary War was fought.

There wasn't much traffic as we started to climb to the bridge. Our outfit took up about half a lane, so drivers were careful not to pass one another when they saw us, which gave us plenty of room. I was able to pay strict attention to Tarzan.

We'd just crossed the bridge and started down the grade on the west side when I heard a horn tooting to our rear. I turned my head and saw two trucks. A small one was trying to pass a big one. It was a fool thing to try, for it left the big truck with no place to go except smack into Tarzan and me.

Thank the Lord, the driver of the big truck was wearing his thinking cap that morning. He feared his brakes would scare Tarzan and send the horse over the bank, so he went into neutral, hoping to turn out and coast by us. Of course, he was also hoping the little truck would give him room.

The close sounds to our rear – horn, swishing tires and motors – caused Tarzan to rear. He whirled and came down with his front legs over the wire cable. Then his hind legs slipped and we went down just as the big truck swerved out and missed us. It was so close the driver thought he had hit us. He slammed on his brakes and skidded to a sideways stop up ahead. The truck blocked both lanes.

The driver came running back to us, and found me upside down and out cold. My feet were still in the stirrups.

The wire cable had held Tarzan's front, and when his rear went down the saddle had slipped. I should have been thrown, but the sudden action had jammed my feet into the stirrups, and I had remained in the saddle more or less. So I ended up under Tarzan's belly.

I was unconscious for only a few minutes. When I came to I was still on the road, my little dog, Depeche Toi, was licking my face, and two men were trying to free my feet. Because of the felt shoes and rubbers I wore, my feet were too big for those stirrups and I'd ride with just my toes sticking in. Now the too big feet were caught in too small stirrups.

Tarzan stood nice as you please while men freed my feet. By that time, quite a crowd had gathered, but the only familiar face I saw belonged to Mr. Flaherty.

"The only place you three are going today is back to the inn," he said.

I seemed to be in one piece, and so did Tarzan. Some of the men helped to unload him and put the gear in Mr. Flaherty's car. Then Tarzan started acting like a wild horse. I couldn't get a foot in the stirrup. I tried leading him, but he reared and lifted me like a feather.

So the dog and I rode back to Chadd's Ford Inn in Mr. Flaherty's car. Tarzan was led back by the strongest man present.

I didn't have to be persuaded to lie down and rest for the balance of the daylight hours. My whole body ached, but it was a small price to pay for my incredible luck. I told myself that I was lucky to be alive, and that the accident had happened in the right place at the right time. I said a prayer at eleven that morning, and it included thanks to the man who had thought of putting those wire cables alongside the road.

I enjoyed lunch in bed. Then the doctor arrived. I'd asked a vet to look Tarzan over. Mr. Flaherty had thought of the doctor for me.

"How do you feel?" the doctor asked.

"Well bruised," I told him. "Otherwise, I'm fine. I don't need a doctor."

"Judging from the report of the accident, you may need ten doctors. I'll take your pulse first." He did, and then said, "I can tell you that you are not in a state of shock."

After that he took my temperature, and examined me. "Nothing broken, but you'll be stiff for days and sore for a week. All I can prescribe is plenty of rest."

"Doctors keep telling me that," I told him.

"And they always will. By the way, I've examined your horse. Nothing to worry about. A few small scratches and a little swelling in one rear ankle. The bone isn't broken. Something hit him there. He can use some rest, too."

"Are you a doctor or a vet?"

"A little of both. I'll drop by tomorrow."

"I won't be here!"

"You'll change your mind," he laughed, and he was right. The next morning I was so stiff and sore that all I wanted out of life was one hot bath after another. I didn't budge from that room until nightfall, and then I was obliged to, having accepted a supper invitation from Mr. Wyeth, the man who did the drawing of Tarzan.

He had several other guests there. The supper was in my honor, although I didn't have to make a speech. Mr. Wyeth showed me a new drawing he had made of Tarzan, with me in the saddle. I judged his picture of me as better than the one I had on the folder I gave out to people, and told him so. I also told him that his work was just as good as some professional artists who sold their drawings for fancy prices in Portland, Maine every summer.

"You should try selling your stuff," I told him, and he promised to think about it.

This is an excerpt from "Last of the Saddle Tramps" by Messanie Wilkins.

Messanie Wilkins and Tarzan.

Chapter 3
Dead Horse Pass
by
Wilfred Skrede

Wilfred Skrede was nineteen in 1941, when the Nazis occupied his homeland of Norway. Determined to reach the training camp of the free Norwegian Air Force located in Toronto, Canada, the daring young man set off across Russia, Siberia, China, Turkestan and India before finally reaching his destination in faraway North America, more than one year later. The most perilous portion of his trip occurred on the infamous Gilgit Road, a hideous bit of trail famous for killing horses and riders alike.

Luckily for Skrede, just prior to his departure from Chinese Turkestan, the British Consul at Kashgar discovered the young adventurer had no equestrian experience. The English diplomat took pity on the Norwegian refugee and offered to give him shelter and a crash course in riding. Skrede's extraordinary run of luck was about to change however.

His brief riding lessons came just in time because the Chinese governor ordered the amateur equestrian explorer escorted out of the country, under the watchful eyes of three armed Chinese soldiers.

With orders not to return to Kashgar, Skrede had only one option, to head for freedom by riding a Turkestani caravan-pony over the infamous 16,000 foot high Dead Horse Pass.

Mr. Shipton sketched the whole route for me; first fourteen days riding to Misgar; then another good week in the Karakorums, through the mountainous Hunza country to Gilgit and from there ten to twelve days more across the western Himalayas to Srinagar in Kashmir, from where there was a motor road to the nearest railway station at Rawalpindi, India.

"The whole road is tough mountainous country," he said, "and even you who come from Norway and are used to mountains will find things there a little difficult. To manage this trip you must be able to ride. Can you?"

The only time I had tried was in my early childhood, when I had clambered up on to the back of an aged farm horse which was so steady that an old woman could have ridden it blindfold. I had to admit despondently that unfortunately I could not ride.

"Okay," said Mr. Shipton, "we'll teach you."

He drew up a program for my days: riding and other training to get me back into shape. And, as he smilingly put it: "I shall see if we can teach you to maltreat my mother tongue a little less."

There can be few places where the distinction between horse and horse is so crass as in Turkestan. You see well groomed bloodhorses so lovely that you quiver with joy at the sight of them and caravan ponies so shabby and emaciated, as to make the most indifferent flinch. There lies a social gulf between the proud Badakshan stallion and the ever famished, everlastingly toiling proletarians of the mountain road.

The policemen's horses looked pretty poor creatures and the one I was to ride no better. However, as it and I were to be buddies for a couple of weeks, I went up to introduce myself. I started by trying to disentangle a bit of its dirty forelock. Sulky and disobliging, it jerked its head away: obviously these horses did not get much in the way of pats or petting.

"Sociable you are certainly not," said I, "but you had better have a name even so. I shall call you Mohammad."

The three soldiers escorting me to the Chinese-Indian border were Khirgiz, stocky, powerful chaps who were thoroughly at home in the mountains. They understood not a word of what I said, and sign language was our only means of conversing.

There was also a small girl going with us. She sat on her horse quite enveloped in a rose-colored quilted kaftan, which allowed only the tip of her turned-up nose to be seen. Thus there were five horses in our caravan as we emerged from Kashgar and set out sedately across the plain.

That first day we got no further than the little cluster of houses at Yapsjan, for one of the horses took ill and there we spent the night in what the Turkomans call a hangar: on a hillside was a rectangular little field, at the top of the slope was a covered ledge on which we slept, below it a half-shelter for the animals.

Throughout the whole of the following day we rode through a uniform countryside where you saw nothing but interminable sand dunes and the dirty-gray bed of a stream with a tamarisk bush here and there. We spent the night in the oasis of Yangi Hissar and then, on the evening of the third day, we reached the little oasis of Igiz Yar.

Here a number of Turkistanis joined us. The policemen got hold of several more horses and on these loaded oats and other provisions for our animals. It was thus quite a good sized caravan of some twenty beasts which left Igiz Yar. From there we could see mountains ahead of us, and it was not long before we were out of the sand dunes and had come into a glen. At the foot of the mountains lay some of the usual mud huts and a few poplar and apricot trees.

The glen was roomy enough at the start: there were green slopes, a few woods here and there and the stream wound along lazy and sluggish. But the glen soon narrowed and it was not long before the stream had whipped itself into a raging torrent.

Slowly the Gilgit Road unfolded. I sat my horse and kept finding it hard to believe my eyes - I don't know what I wouldn't have given to have had a camera. Soon the road took to a narrow shelf in the mountainside 200 feet or so above the foaming torrent, with the rock dropping sheer beneath it and rising almost equally sheer for over a thousand feet on either side, then it descended down a narrow ravine to the valley floor and some rapids. Somehow or other we managed to get across, and then we had to clamber up along another narrow shelf. Of course there were many places where you could not ride but had to lead your horse behind you.

The first time we crossed the river I thought that my travels were to end there in that devilish hole, that in a moment or two the entire caravan would be sent swirling and shrieking down the rapids. But the policemen just went slap in so that the spray spurted up round them. Their wild shouts were nothing to go by - that was just something that went with the scene, though perhaps at that moment they were more savage than usual. I realized that there was nothing much I could do about it except to trust to Mohammad. And Mohammad followed the horse in front of him without an instant's hesitation.

I had to pull my feet out of the stirrups for the grayish-yellow water was foaming close under the brute's belly. I could feel that Mohammad was fighting against the pressure of the current for all he was worth and actually stamping his hooves down to get a hold on the uneven bottom. We got across all right.

So it continued throughout the day. I believe we crossed that torrent every five hundred yards and I learned to admire the shaggy Turkoman horses for their ability to make their way whether fording a rushing river or climbing a steep ravine. They must be the most sure-footed creatures in the world. I know that here and there in the ravines and gullies lay the skeletons of horses to show that many of those maltreated and abused drudges had succumbed while plying the Gilgit Road; but all went well for us and I had many grateful thoughts to Mr. Shipton for having taught me to ride.

Gradually the ground began to rise more steeply and by evening we were fairly high up the mountain. We spent the night in the open. I was stiff in every limb and as tired as could be but nevertheless I tackled the pepper and mutton with a voracious appetite. The view was magnificent but it could not hold me for long – I was too tired for that.

The following day we continued. At first across an upland plateau, then down into another valley, where we again had to negotiate a ford which, if possible, was even worse than any we had had before.

Having labored through a narrow bluffy glen we emerged on to another plateau. There we met a camel caravan and I wondered what would have happened if we had encountered it in the narrowest part of the glen?

There were various kinds of birds up there and we saw herds of odd looking goats and sheep; some had horns like giant corkscrews. Besides these, there were innumerable marmots which sat in the mouths of their holes and hissed at us.

Then we began to encounter the Gilgit Road's own special sign posts; the half eaten bodies of horses. Grayish-white vultures swung round us on heavy wings.

At one point my policemen sought variety in a little hunting. We had put up some white birds about the size of a capercailzie[3] and the guns came into action. They were not very good shots and brought nothing down, all the same it developed into a lively hunt which showed what good horsemen they were and demonstrated the incredible skill of these horses on rough ground.

We came to a place called Aktala where there was a cluster of round felt tents, yurts or kibitkas, as the Khirgiz call them. Thick felt rugs are laid over a framework of thin wooden stakes – about the thickness of a fishing rod – and tied with cords round the outside. These yurts looked quite substantial and were indeed fairly roomy. The floors inside consist of several layers of rugs laid over a thick layer of moss and the fact that there were plenty of lice in these rugs was a thing I could do nothing about unfortunately.

It was devilishly cold in Aktala but the mountain air was pure and fresh and how lovely it was to be free of the myriad flies of Turkestan.

Down in the valleys I had seen quite a number of woods, mostly fir but now we were above the treeline and there was nothing but bare expanses and screes and huge rocks to be seen. To the west we could see the first of the 22,000 to 23,000 foot giants which flank the Gilgit Road - snowcapped Mustagh Ata, father of the mountains and sovereign of the Sarikol.

It was in these wilds that we met yaks for the first time. Yaks can only live in the high mountains, above ten thousand feet. They have heavy bodies, short legs and long straggly hair which sweeps down to their heels and makes them look like hay-cocks perched among the stones. Their appearance was terrifying and for all their great size they hopped about the mountainside as easily and lightly as any goat.

---

[3] Editor's note: A large black grouse, about the size of an North American turkey.

Then we came to Kashka Su and there too were many yurts. Otherwise there was just the bare savage mountain: rugged and as cold as charity. There was no getting away from the fact that it was a draughty and dreary spot but all the same I felt more at home there than among the flies and dust in the intolerable heat of the plains. We were allowed into one of the yurts, got a fire going with dried yak dung and were relatively comfortable.

Shortly after leaving Kashka Su the road became ghastly: long, steep slopes that pumped the guts out of you and no sooner had we surmounted that and got up on a plateau than we had to slither down precipitous bluffs on the other side. After that we plunged straight into another glen as wild and as narrow as any we had traversed and through it ran yet another swift and fierce torrent. Again we began those nerve-racking fordings every few hundred yards, then the road began to climb once more. What faced us now was one of the worst bits of the entire trip: the ascent to the Chichiklik Pass.

Chichiklik lies somewhat over fifteen thousand feet above sea level and is the second highest pass on the Gilgit Road. Only the dreaded Mintaka Pass is higher and worse. The descent from that Dead Horse pass was bad enough, but it was not so ghastly as the climb up.

The road wound its way upwards in an infinity of bends , then into a gigantic scree of boulders as large as houses. Along the whole pass there are dark-brown splodges on the stones. Once they were fresh steaming blood. Each drop was a message left from the trembling horses that had foundered there.

Our horses had a ghastly time of it. Even though we dismounted and walked, they still had the baggage to carry and it was obvious that the great height and the thinness of the air affected them worse than us. It was pitiable to watch them toiling up step by step, then suddenly halting with all four legs straddled and their flanks heaving in an effort to get air. The skeletons of horses lay at frequent intervals and an occasional small cairn, some with a horses' tail as a decoration, proclaimed that there lay the mortal remains of a man.

Pity for a horse, however, is an unknown sentiment on the Chichiklik Pass.

I thought I would retch when the Turkomans began jabbing their horses on the muzzle with sharp iron spikes so that the blood ran. I was told that this was not cruelty to the animals but a humane blood-letting which helps the poor brutes to support the rarity of the atmosphere ! Perhaps it is but it looks too horrible for words.

For hundreds and hundreds of years caravans have been passing between Kashmir and Kashgar. To many people that is a nice romantic thought but not to those who have crossed the cruel Chichiklik Pass and had a glimpse of the hell which that trading route has been for thousands of tormented ponies who just had to toil and endure it all and had no Allah to call upon.

This is an excerpt from "Across the Roof of the World" by Wilfred Skrede.

Caravan horses crossing the Chichiklik Pass

Chapter 4
Ride A White Horse
by
William Holt

Equestrian stories are full of adventures, hardships, danger and drama. Yet the curious story of William Holt and his cart horse, Trigger, is one of the most inspiring equestrian travel tales. After rescuing the gelding from slaughter and then nursing him back to health, the 67-year-old Holt and his aging mount set out in 1964 on an incredible 9,000 mile, non-stop journey through Europe.

The resultant trip saw them sleeping out in the rough without a tent for more than 400 nights. Together they faced great hardships, suffering through storms, floods and whirlwinds. At one point in their travels the aging gypsies were marooned on a ledge and nearly drowned by the raging sea.

Because of these shared dangers, Holt and Trigger maintained a legendary bond that touched people's hearts. An Italian princess had jewels set in one of Trigger's old shoes. They were guests of the Queen of England in London.

Holt however was never tempted to rank himself above his horse. He opted to sleep with Trigger on the grass outside elegant castle walls, content to ignore the feather beds offered by royalty. Together they rubbed shoulders with peasants and princes and remind us of why we ride over the hill looking for that next elusive adventure.

We were nearing Rome after riding the whole length of the Via Aurelia.

Via Aurelia ...... how can I ever forget you now?

What a long way !

What a long time !

What thoughts, what dreams, living and sleeping along this fabled road. The long straight levels, the steep climbs, the curves, the corniches, the galleries, the umbrella pines shading us from the hot sun, the snow and ice, the rain, the marble, the thundering traffic.

Will Trigger ever forget those heavy lorries and trailers?

Riding, they brushed my knees, walking by the side of Trigger I stepped back and squeezed against him as the big lorries approached with headlights blazing. Great, long, twelve-wheelers, towing trailers, looming like houses, nearly running over us. The trailers have no headlights. As the shadowy lorry passes, the trailer comes afterwards with a shock in the darkness. Between the lorry and its trailer are dim lights which cast a beam of light across the road. This beam comes like a scythe in the night towards us. I have sometimes put my hand in front of my face and shut my eyes, as this scythe of light comes at speed towards us.

The din of these "heavies" will echo in my mind forever.

So many of them, and all through the night, sometimes a procession of them coming round curves, mounting gradients with groaning gears, descending hairpin bends with squeaking brakes.

A nightmare of modern traffic.

And yet, although we had not then left the Via Aurelia, I already felt stirring deep within me that affection, that longing that torments me now when I think of our ride. I would not have missed it for the world. Even Trigger, now that it is over, has behind him the grand experience of traveling the way the chariots went. We were happy most of the time.

Trigger knows how happy.

Now we were nearing Rome, the eternal city. Trigger is not interested in history, although his horse ancestors helped to make it. I saw things that took my thoughts back a long way, passing through that grave, mysterious landscape. I saw the smile on the lips of a young woman in a mural at Tarquinia, an Etruscan smile from 300 BC.

When I passed a dump of crashed cars I thought of that smile. The Etruscans knew that all things in this world are subject to Time, which becomes their fate.

After we had passed through Civiravecchia the weather became warmer and that night I slept uncovered. I was so tired I fell down asleep while unrolling my blanket. That was near the 35 kilometer stone as we neared Rome.

On 31st March, 1965 we halted at the 22 kilometer stone near the river Arrone. We had been on the road eight months. I wanted to do a bit of spit and polish before our entry into Rome. All around us were grass-covered low hummocks of the Roman campagna. Trigger was eating his oats while I snatched a quick meal of cheese and olives and lit a Tuscan cigar. It was then that I decided to stop there all day and rest overnight and ride into Rome the next morning.

Roma !

At last the name stood before us on an iron post. A group of people were standing there at the boundary to welcome us, including a priest. It was the beginning of the most extraordinary experience of my life. For Trigger too, it was the commencement of an adventure of extreme contrasts, the threshold of romance.

When Trigger and I first met he had only one shoe.

One of his shoes is now set with precious stones in an Italian palace.

I knew nobody in Rome.

In Paris we had a letter of introduction. Paris welcomed us. We stayed a whole week.

In Rome we stayed two months.

Paris held us by wonder and excitement.

Rome held us with love.

Ah ! When I first saw this white horse and made my wish did I really believe that it would come true? I certainly did not imagine then that I should become a vagabond with a horse in the streets of London, Paris and Rome. During the whole of my stay in Rome I slept in the open with my horse, but under what exceptional circumstances ! Much of the time I slept in a Roman street on a patch of wild grass that apparently belonged to nobody, lay down with Trigger, lulled to sleep by the all-night traffic, adored by schoolboys, cafe kiosk keepers, petrol pump attendants, beggars, street-sweepers. Some of the time I left a loaded table after dining with an Italian princess, waited on by a butler in white-and-gold livery wearing white gloves, to lie down with Trigger on the grass outside the palace. When I declined the kind offer of a luxurious bedroom and bathroom I was told that I the first guest in history of that ancient noble family to sleep instead with his horse under the stars.

But Trigger knows why I slept with him on our long journey.

There are no secrets so close as that between a rider and his horse.

The Romans who met us at the boundary showed me the way into the city. Where the Via Aurelia meets the Via Gregono VII I saw a stretch of grass behind a hoarding where we returned that first night to sleep.

First we made for St. Peter's square, then to the bank of the Tiber river. The striking view of the Castel Sant'Angelo with its bridge seen from the left bank inspired my first picture in Rome. I rode down next day when the sun was rising and did a pen and ink sketch. The east side of the castle was flooded with light, the angels on the beautiful Ponte Sant'Angelo were dazzling white, the arches of the bridge, dating from Hadrian, cast long shadows.

While I was sketching an Italian wanted to buy the picture. He offered me 7,000 lire.

"But I haven't finished it yet," I said, not wanting to part with it while it was still a living, pulsating piece of my heart.

"When will you have it finished? Where can I meet you?"

I told him where I slept and that night he brought 7,000 lire. Not a bad start.

On riding along the bank of the river I had seen how the winged figure of a woman, with arm outstretched bearing a laurel crown, appeared to be taking off in flight from the budding trees. The sun-drenched, awakening trees cast long shadows in the rising sun. I rode down next morning to do this picture, which to me after our long hard winter, was the very embodiment of "Spring on the banks of the Tiber," and I was already calling it that.

With a thrill I saw it again. Then suddenly in my excitement I saw in front of me on the pavement the shadow of my horse as well.

I hesitated.

Could I permit this other shadow to come in?

Why not?

It balanced wonderfully against the sweeping figure of the winged statue in the sky. I sketched the shadows there and then.

The junction of the ways where Trigger and I slept was called Circonvallazione Aurelia. On one side of us was a rather rickety cafe kiosk built mainly of trellis, on the other side, some distance away, was a petrol station. In the morning the sun shone through the trellis and the silk parasols of women sitting with their coffee.

Attendants from the petrol pump drew water for Trigger from a public water tap across the road, schoolboys got through a hole in the high netting to gather lucerne on a building lot owned by the Vatican, for Trigger to eat. At night the petrol station closed but the kiosk remained open late, illuminated by strings of colored bulbs. Fernando Carinci, the kiosk owner, regaled me with wine and refused payment, and there was Alvaro, a young man who helped him, a girl, Autonietta, who frequented the neighborhood, and rascally Stracchino who shaved half his mustache off to make me laugh. I sketched portraits of all these. And there was a little prostitute who when passing used to shout to me, "Americano, Americano ! I love you. Gimme million lire !"

Trigger loved Rome because nobody turned him off the grass as they had in London. Each morning on our way down the avenue Via Gregono VII he grazed on the wide verge between the two lanes of the roadway, and he always had his drink at the stone trough by the wall of the Vatican City. There is abundant pure drinking water in Rome, and Romans, young and old, put their mouths under the taps and fountains in the streets.

One morning on our way down the Via Gregono VII a young man caught up with me in his car. He had come from the Italian princess Angelica del Drago with an invitation for Trigger and myself to stay with her at her palace. A young lady called Deana Frosini would meet me on horseback and show me the way. It was a lovely ride, the trees budding, the birds singing, and Trigger was ravished by the company of another horse. The heads of six more horses craned over the half doors of loose-boxes on our arrival. An elegant brunette came towards me holding out her hand.

"You are the principessa?" I asked.

She nodded and I presented Trigger to her. She made quite a fuss over him, asked me a lot of questions about his background, fed him sugar lumps and then asked me if I would do something for her as a favor. She wanted me to give her one of the shoes that Trigger had worn down the Via Aurelia. It was a small favor but I was proud that she had asked.

"I shall send it to a jeweler," she said, "and have it set with stones as an ornament here. And in return I will buy Trigger a new set of shoes, and we must have the best farrier in Rome."

That evening I dined with the princess and the Italian Prince Giovanni, as well as the Bourbon prince, whose grandfather was once king of Naples and Sicily before being deposed. Trigger meanwhile was happy in a field of luscious grass into which another horse had been let loose for company.

This was the beginning of a happy interlude and a rest which lasted many weeks. Sometimes the chauffeur drove me into Rome, sometimes I rode Trigger. The police would not let me set up my easel in the streets so I often sketched from my saddle. If I returned late from Rome the princess would tell me next day that she had left her bedroom window open to listen for the footsteps of Trigger.

We stayed in Rome until June.

I managed to build up a nice little fund by the sale of my pictures, bought myself new jodhpurs, jacket, shoes and a Panama hat. In the streets of Rome not only the Romans but also the tourists were interested in Trigger and I answered questions in many languages. Sometimes I would sit outside a cafe while Trigger ate his oats and I would eat a tramezzino, a delicious Roman sandwich, and drink a cappuccino-coffee with a dash of milk in a doll's half cup (Romans are drinking these all day).

Trigger watched me. Even when his nosebag was on, his eyes were always on me.

Priests invited me to lunch, a professor from Iceland who was recuperating in Rome after an illness invited me to dinner, and one day in the Via Vittoria, a young woman came to pat Trigger. She had a brilliantly colored silk scarf over her arm, was carrying books, a beaded handbag and flowers – Trigger tried to eat the flowers – and she was wearing fashionable white lace stockings. After a chat she gave me her card which bore a coronet, Michelina di Vinciguerra, a marchesa from Foggia, and invited me to have coffee with her each morning in the Piazza Largo St. Carlo. She brought me copies of Italian songs and sang them to me in a low contralto voice.

What a variety of ecclesiastical costumes in the streets – nuns, priests, monks of different religious orders, robes and gowns blowing in the wind; there was always a wind blowing while we were in Rome. I sketched these in movement, on horseback, and the picturesque carabiniere. In the streets was a nonchalant, tolerant atmosphere, traffic giving way to my horse, police often halting traffic for us to pass. Whenever we stopped the Romans gathered round us smiling and passing ingenious remarks, unaffected like children, and nobody in a hurry. Watching me sketch they would exclaim, "Bello, bello (good, good)."

Trigger knew his way about Rome. He could find his way to the stretch of wild grass at the Circonvallazione Aurelia where we slept if I dropped the reins in the evening in the middle of Rome. If I wanted to go to our other home-from-home in Rome I had only to turn to the road to San Cosimato or even mention it and he would find his way to the Tenuta del Drago. Sometimes we rode up to the Villa Borghese where Trigger could graze and roll on the grass. When we first arrived in Rome in April the cafes, bars and shops were stocked with sweets, chocolates, and dolls for Easter. Italians have a sweet tooth, there are always more sweets than savory confections displayed in bars. Trigger's tooth is sweet and he enjoyed Italian sweets.

As the weeks went by both Trigger and I became more and more settled in Rome. The city had received us in a wonderful way. One day a man came up to me in the street and said simply, "Rome loves you. Don't go away."

But when June came we were ready to ride across Italy to the Adriatic Sea. The hot weather had not yet arrived and I had heard of snow still lingering in the Apennines mountains that blocked our way. A French guest dining with the princess at dinner said that he had come through flooded roads in his car on the way from Naples.

Freak weather again!

Yet Trigger and I had experienced plenty of this. But Princess Angelica urged me to stay in Rome.

"Trigger's already done enough for one horse in a lifetime," she said.

I had had a vet look at Trigger's foreleg on my arrival in Rome. He had said that his previous injury was not serious and it would do him no harm to continue on our journey after a rest. Now I judged him quite fit.

"Chi va piano va lontano (He who journeys slowly travels far)," I told the princess.

A champagne party was given when I saddled Trigger and said "Goodbye."

The Princess Angelica and a dozen guests stood on the castle steps and toasted Trigger and me. My glass was being refilled by the Bourbon Prince even after I had mounted. As we rode away I felt a little sad and Trigger stopped several times and looked back.

The princess and her party, as well as the servants of the Tenuta del Drago, were waving to us and all the horses had their heads out of the loose-boxes.

It was a sad moment for both of us. Our friends waved until we were out of sight.

We had to ride through the centre of Rome, across the Piazza del Popolo to reach the Via Flaminia. The Romans could see by my load and the bag of oats across my saddle that I was leaving. Many came to shake hands and to touch Trigger one last time, and a man said, "You are original. We love you."

Joining the Via Flaminia, we headed north for the first time since leaving Yorkshire, England.

This is an excerpt from "Ride a White Horse" by William Holt.

William Holt and Trigger

Chapter 5
An Instinctive Passion
by
Charles Darwin

In contemplating the brilliant intellectual achievements of the past, Charles Darwin's name is often mentioned. Whether you agree with his famous "Theory of Evolution" or not, Darwin's impact on the course of modern events cannot be denied. His was a life whose resonance is still being felt around the globe. It goes against the grain of common perception to think of this scientific titan galloping over the pampas of Argentina, exploring volcanic islands on horseback, and lying down to rest on the bosom of the earth with his horse nearby. Yet Darwin's diaries tell the story of not just a naturalist exploring the world searching for answers, they also reveal the inner man, the Long Rider who reveled in the freedom of riding on three continents, South America, Australia, and Africa. For as these varied diary entries explain, Charles Darwin the Scientist, soon discovered that when you are a Long Rider you often find astonishing acts of kindness awaiting you out on the long gray road to adventure.

BRAZIL
Rio de Janeiro
April 6th, 1832

The day has been frittered away in obtaining the passports for my expedition into the interior. It is never very pleasant to submit to the insolence of men in office. But the prospect of visiting wild forests tenanted by beautiful birds, monkeys, sloths, and alligators will make any Naturalist lick the dust even from the foot of a Brazilian.

April 8th, 1832

At 9 o'clock I joined my party at Praia Grande, a village on the opposite side of the Bay. We were six in number and consisted of Mr. Patrick Lennon, a regular Irishman, who when the Brazils were first opened to the English made a large fortune by selling spectacles. About eight years since he purchased a tract of forest country on the Macae river and put an English agent over it. Communication is so difficult that from that time to the present he has been unable to obtain any remittances. After many delays Mr. Patrick resolved in person to visit his estate. It was easily arranged that I should be a companion and in many respects it will be an excellent opportunity for seeing the country and its inhabitants. Mr. Lennon has resided in Brazil 20 years and was in consequence well qualified to obtain information.

He was accompanied by his nephew, a sharp youngster, following the steps of his Uncle and making money. Thirdly came Mr. Laurie, a well informed clever Scotchman, a selfish unprincipled man, by trade partly Slave-merchant, partly swindler. He brought a friend, a Mr. Gosling, an apprentice to a Druggist. A black boy as guide and myself completed the party, and the wilds of Brazil have seldom seen a more extraordinary and quixotic set of adventurers.

Our first stage was very interesting; the day was powerfully hot and as we passed through the woods, everything was still, excepting the large and brilliant butterflies, which lazily fluttered about. The view seen when crossing the hills behind Praia Grande is most sublime and picturesque. The colours were intense and the prevailing tint a dark blue; the sky and calm waters of the bay vied with each other in splendour. After passing through some cultivated country we entered a forest which in the grandeur of all its parts could not be exceeded. I was utterly at a loss how sufficiently to admire this scene.

We continued riding for some hours; for the last miles the road was intricate, it passed through a desert waste of marshes and lagoons. The scene by the dimmed light of the moon was most desolate; a few fire-flies flitted by us and the solitary snipe as it rose uttered its plaintive cry; and the distant and sullen roar of the sea scarcely broke the stillness of the night. We arrived at the Venda and were very glad to lie down on the straw mats.

April 9th, 1832

Having been 10 hours on horseback, I never cease to wonder at the amount of labour which these horses are capable of enduring.

April 11th, 1832

Travelled on till it was dark, felt miserably faint and exhausted; I often thought I should have fallen off my horse.

April 12th, 1832

The next morning I cured myself by eating cinnamon and drinking port wine.

April 14th, 1832

Started at midday for Mr. Lennon's estate. The road passed through a vast extent of forest in which we saw many beautiful birds. We slept in a Fazenda a league from our journey's end. The agent received us hospitably and was the only Brazilian I had seen with a good expression. The slaves appeared miserably overworked and badly clothed.

April 15th, 1832

We were obliged to have a black man clear the way with a sword. The woods in this neighbourhood contain several forms of vegetation which I had not seen before, some elegant tree ferns and a grass like papyrus.

When we arrived at the estate there was a most violent and disagreeable quarrel between Mr. Lennon and his agent, Mr. Cowper. During Mr. Lennon's quarrel with his agent, he threatened to sell at the public auction an illegitimate child to whom Mr. Cowper was much attached. Also, he put into execution taking all the women and children from their husbands and selling them separately at the market in Rio. How strange and inexplicable is the effect of habit and interest. Against such facts how weak are the arguments of those who maintain that slavery is a tolerable evil.

April 20th, 1832

Returned by the old route to Campos Novos. The ride was very tiresome, passing over a heavy and scorching sand. Whilst swimming our horses over the St. Joao river, we had some danger and difficulty. The animals became exhausted and we had to contend with two drunken mulattos in a boat. We arrived back at Rio in the evening and were obliged to sleep on a bed of Indian corn.

ARGENTINA
Baia Blanca
September 7th, 1832

There were several of the wild Gaucho cavalry waiting to see us land. They formed by far the most savage, picturesque group I ever beheld. I should have fancied myself in the middle of Turkey by their dresses. Round their waists they had bright coloured shawls forming a petticoat, beneath which were fringed drawers. Their boots were very singular. They are made from the hide of the hock joint of horses' hind legs, so that it is a tube with a bend in it. This they put on fresh and thus drying on their legs is never again removed. Their spurs are enormous, the rowels being one to two inches long. They all wore the Poncho, which is a large shawl with a hole in the middle for the head. Thus equipped with sabres and short muskets, they were mounted on powerful horses.

The men themselves were far more remarkable than their dresses. The greater were half Spaniard and Indian, some of each pureblood and some black. The Indians, whilst gnawing bones of beef, looked as though they were half-recalled wild beasts. No painter ever imagined so wild a set of expressions. As the evening was closing in, it was determined not to return to the vessel. So we all mounted behind the gauchos and started a hand gallop for the fort. This place has been attacked several times by large bodies of Indians. The war is carried on in the most barbarous manner. The Indians torture all their prisoners, and the Spaniards shoot theirs. The Commandante's son was taken some time since by the Indians. After being bound, the Indian children prepared to kill him with nails and small knives, a refinement in cruelty I never heard of. A Cacique Indian then said that the next day more people would be present and there would be more sport, so the execution was deferred and in the night he escaped.

September 8th, 1832

The Gauchos were very civil and took us to the only spot where there was any chance of water. It was interesting seeing these hardy people fully equipped for an expedition. They sleep on the bare ground, and as they travel get their food. Already they had killed a puma, the tongue of which was the only part they kept; also an ostrich, these they catch by two heavy balls fastened to the ends of a long thong. Having given our friends some dollars they left us in high good humour and assured us that they would someday bring us a live lion. We then returned on board.

PATAGONIA
Rio Colorado
August 11th, 1833

We started early in the morning, but owing to some horses being stolen, we were obliged to travel slowly. Shortly after passing the first spring, we came in sight of the famous tree which the Indians reverence as the altar of their God, Walleechu. It is situated on a high part of the plain, and hence is a landmark visible at a great distance. Being winter, the tree had no leaves, but in their place were countless threads by which various offerings had been suspended. Cigars, bread, meat, pieces of cloth etc. To complete the scene, the tree was surrounded by the bleached bones of horses slaughtered as sacrifices. All Indians of every age and sex make their offerings; they then think that their horses will not tire and that they shall be prosperous.

About two leagues from this very curious tree we halted for the night. At this instant, an unfortunate cow was spied by the lynx-eyed Gauchos. Off we set in chase, and in a few minutes she was dragged in by the lazo and slaughtered. Here we had the four necessaries for life "en el campo," pasture for the horses, water (only a muddy puddle), meat and firewood. The Gauchos were in high spirits at finding all these luxuries, and we soon set to work at the poor cow. There is high enjoyment in the independence of the Gauchos' life: to be able at any moment to pull up your horse and say, "Here we will pass the night."

The death-like stillness of the plain, the dogs keeping watch, the gypsy group of Gauchos making their beds around the fire, has left in my mind a strongly-marked picture of this night which will not soon be forgotten.

CHILE
Navedad
September 19th, 1834

I felt during the day very unwell and from this time to the end of October did not recover. Rode but a short distance and was then obliged to rest. Our course now lay directly to Valparaiso, Chile. We found a rich Haciendero, who received us in his house close to the sea. At night I was exceedingly exhausted but had the uncommon luck of obtaining some clean straw for my bed. I was amused afterwards by reflecting how truly comparative all comfort is. If I had been in England and very unwell, clean straw and stinking horse blankets would have been thought a very miserable bed.

Potrero Seco
June 11th, 1835

Rode for 12 hours without stopping, till we reached the Hacienda of Potrero Seco. I was heartily glad. The whole journey is a source of anxiety to see how fast you can cross the Traversia desert. To all appearances however the horses were quite fresh and no one could have told they had not eaten for the last 55 hours.

AUSTRALIA
Sydney
January 19th, 1836

I hired a man and two horses to take me to Bathurst, a village about hundred and twenty miles in the interior. By this means I hoped to get a general appearance of the country. The first stage took us through Paramatta, a small country town. The roads were excellent and were much frequented by carriages. I also met two stage coaches. In all these respects there was a most close resemblance to England, perhaps the number of Ale-houses was here in excess. The parties of convicts, who have committed some trifling offence in this country, appeared the least like England. They were dressed in yellow and grey clothes and were working in irons under the charge of sentrys with loaded guns.

At sunset by good fortune a party of a score of the Aborginal Blacks passed by, each carrying, in their accustomed manner, a bundle of spears and other weapons. Their countenances were good humoured and pleasant.

January 20th, 1836

This day we had an instance of the sirocco-like wind of Australia which comes from the parched deserts of the interior. While riding I was not fully aware how exceedingly high the temperature was. Later I heard the thermometer out of doors stood at 119 degrees and in a room in a closed house at 96 degrees. It was during that late afternoon that we came into view of the town of Bathurst.

The officers all seemed very weary of this place and I am not surprised at all, as it must be to them a place of exile.

AFRICA
Cape Colony
June 4th, 1836

I hired a couple of horses and a young Hottentot groom to accompany me as a guide. He spoke English very well and was most tidily dressed. He wore a long coat, beaver hat and white gloves.

Our first day's ride was to the village of Paarl, situated forty miles from the Cape Town. Even at this short distance from the coast there were several very pretty little birds. If a person could not find amusement in observing the animals and plants, there was very little else during the day to interest him.

ISLAND OF TERCEIRA
Angra
September 9th, 1836

We crossed the Tropic of Cancer and in the morning we were off the island of Terceira. The island is moderately lofty and has a rounded outline with hills evidently of volcanic origin. The land is well cultivated and small hamlets are scattered in all parts.

The next day the Consul kindly lent me his horse and furnished me with guides to a spot in the centre of the island, which was described as an active volcano.

When we reached the crater the bottom was traversed by several large fissures out of which small jets of steam issued as from the cracks in the boiler of a steam engine. It is said that flames once issued from the cracks.

ENGLAND
Falmouth
October 2nd, 1836

After a tolerably short passage, but with some heavy weather, we came to an anchor at Falmouth. To my surprise and shame I confess the first sight of the shores of England inspired me with no warmer feelings than if it had been a miserable Portuguese settlement. The same night, and a dreadful stormy one it was, I took the stage for Shrewsbury.

In conclusion, I am sure the pleasure of living in the open air, with the sky for a roof, and the ground for a table, is part of an instinctive passion. It is the savage returning to his wild and native habits. I do not doubt every traveller must remember the glowing sense of happiness, from the simple consciousness of breathing in a foreign clime, where the civilized man has seldom or never trod.

It appears to me that nothing can be more improving to a young naturalist than a journey in distant countries. The excitement from the novelty of objects, and the chance of success, stimulates him on to activity.

Travelling ought to teach him that he will discover how many truly good natured people there are with whom he never before had, nor ever again will have any further communication, yet who are ready to offer him the most disinterested assistance.

These extracts can be found in "The Works of Charles Darwin – Diary of the Voyage of the Beagle, Volume One," edited by Nora Barlow, published in 1987 by the New York University Press.

Chapter 6
A Journey to Simplify Life
By
DC Vision

Not only had DC Vision never made an equestrian journey, he had never even mounted a horse. Yet that didn't stop the young man from Maine from setting out in 1991 on what would become the longest American equestrian journey of the late 20t[h] Century. Mounted on a loving, if unlikely, Shire mare named Louise, the would-be Long Rider soon discovered that riding 14,000 miles had opened the door to inner and outer explorations.

I didn't know it at the time, but my life was about to change profoundly. There was nothing extraordinary about the reporter's interview. It was essentially the same interview I had given over five hundred times. The same questions, and the same rote answers. Looking back, I know I had crossed some imaginary line. I was no longer speaking to the newspaper's readers, but finally allowing myself to be honest. It may cost me the interview, I thought, but I was tired of portraying myself as what the external world expected of me.

The question the young woman asked was, "So why did you undertake such a long journey in the first place?" I looked at her and asked whether she wanted the rehearsed answer, or the truth. Even she sensed that something different was taking place between us, and flipped to a fresh page on her notebook.

I took the trip because I wanted to prove to myself that I was still alive. My life no longer made any sense to me. I had everything that the television had told me for 25 years that I needed in order to be happy. But I felt like an M&M... I had this wonderful candy-coated shell, but there wasn't any chocolate inside of me. I didn't have any noticeable depth, I guess. I had become little more than a consumer, and I couldn't face another 25 years living like that.

"I was waking up every Monday morning wishing it were Friday, and soon realized that I was rushing away five out of every seven days. And I was a real stress junkie. I wasn't happy unless the pace at work was frantic. I was up to four and a half packs of cigarettes a day, 70 pounds overweight, and I didn't care if I was shortening my life. It's a slow form of suicide, and there are many of us out there who don't realize that."

A typical interview would last about 15 minutes. That interview at a county fairground in southern Idaho lasted six hours, including a large pizza. She even returned the next day with supplies for my journey, and heartfelt thanks for inspiring her to follow some of her unrealized dreams. From that day forward I have never told anyone what they wanted to hear, and have found it impossible to engage in small talk (or superficial talk).

The journey referred to was the second longest horseback ride in the U.S.A. in recorded history. It began in 1991 when I dropped out of the rat race, purchased a Shire draft horse, and logged in nearly 14,000 miles over the next four years and two months. What made such a bold move more astounding, was that I had never ridden a horse prior to undertaking the trip. I chose an unlikely ride on a draft horse, but wanted something that matched my disposition; in other words, liked to eat and refused to run. Louise was perfect, going the distance that a more suitable choice probably wouldn't have.

The final 14 months my horse Louise and I did alone, but the first three years were spent with a dear friend, Tracy Paine (now a resident and student in Washington state). We had planned on marrying when we reached the Pacific Ocean, but after reflecting upon it, discovered that our long-term goals were divergent. We still keep in touch several times a month by mail or phone calls. She rode her Saddlebred horse Dawn for the three years she was with me.

We had a variety of animals with us, usually strays, that would join up until we could find them suitable homes. There was Skidder, Tracy's Newfoundland-mix dog that paced from New Hampshire to Florida with us, only to be eaten by alligators there. There was Myles, a yellow Lab mix who decided to join up in North Carolina. He traveled 6,000 miles with us to Oregon, where we finally found him a suitable home. I never really clicked with Myles. He was a real strange one. He was always sitting in an open spot staring up at the sky, as if waiting for the mother ship (UFO) to come and get him.

The weather was rarely kind to us. We got trapped by a hurricane the fifth day of our trip in a cemetery in Massachusetts. It was 104 degrees in Washington, D.C. and only 8° in Tallahassee, Fla. It rained the whole way, it seemed, aside from a surprise snow storm in June in Montana. It rained so often that the press had dubbed me "The Rainman", a title that sent drought-stricken farmers in Utah to the fairgrounds I was staying at, bearing gifts, and asking me to please stick around. They hadn't seen rain in three years, until a black cloud followed me into town.

We camped out at every place imaginable, from zoos to jails, city parks, inner cities, remote outback, and all points in between. It was one of the unusual side effects of the trip, to wake up and take several minutes to remember what state we were in, let alone what town. It took almost a year to cross Texas, and about the same to get from southern to northern California.

The people were friendliest in the Midwest, and the most unfriendly in the southeast. Denver was the best large city for horseback tourism. We also rode through the downtowns of Philadelphia, Houston, San Antonio, Phoenix, San Diego, Seattle, and even took a picture of the White House in Washington, D.C., when the Secret Service allowed us to ride through the Presidential Rose Garden so we could get from the back of the building to the front.

I was, in total, interviewed by more than 600 newspapers, magazines, and special interest publications. We appeared nearly 100 times on television, including the NBC Nightly News with Tom Brokaw, as well as countless radio interviews. The media coverage helped us to get donations of money, food, and supplies, as well as some great invitations to stay with folks. As we weren't independently wealthy, the entire trip was funded by private donations. We refused to take sponsors.

In writing this, it is not my intention to get into much detail of the trip. For that I could write several books. I wrote this article (July - 1999) because this month it is four years since I last saddled Louise up. I also wanted to share a chapter of my life with my friends and family here in Maine. I hoped to find out what subtle changes such a journey had made in me. I was surprised to discover how much of my present day life was based on the personal growth I experienced those 50 months through 33 states.

You have to bear in mind that the journey wasn't about high adventure (although there was plenty of it); it was about discovering what was important in life. It was about reclaiming those day-to-day things that we all take for granted, such as shelter, warm food, a hot shower and true friendship. After meeting nearly a million people, I can assure you that these "luxuries" aren't as universal as you may think. I can remember Tracy and me thinking we had discovered the Holy Grail in the West because we had finally saved enough money to buy a hotplate, and were going to be able to have hot meals for a change.

One of the most enduring, and endearing, habits that I developed on the trip was to witness the world going to sleep each night, then waking the next morning. Today I spend an hour or so every dawn listening to nature waking up, and repeat the same contemplative exercise every dusk. It is a gift that I give myself each day – a time out from life's ambitious addictions. On the trip it was especially poignant when we were camped at a city or town park. I was determined to witness the final sound of the day of that particular town, and be witness to the next day's initial activity.

This discipline may seem a bit strange in a culture driven by the necessitous activity of doers, but until you witness dawn and dusk in silent contemplation, you have no idea how desultory your life has become. I can recall a day in

Kansas that I was increasingly disturbed by a deafening sound, and when I focused my attention on it, was surprised to discover it was silence. Today I search out that same silence. The fact is, I'm one of those rare people who isn't afraid to be alone with his thoughts.

The other gift the trip afforded me was simplicity. I have remained very faithful to the reason I undertook the journey in the first place – a need to keep my life simple. Undertaking such a trip brings into stark reality that there are few things that we really need in life, aside from food, shelter, and friends. I know that I will never return to that place, in debt, where my possessions owned me. As my need list was established, and my want list was reduced to simple terms, that 40-hour work week became replaced with two days of work, and five days of leisure time to pursue intellectual and spiritual self-education.

Of course I am blessed with special circumstances, such as living with a parent at my age, and enjoying good health. I'm still not certain if a stress-free life can be achieved, but I do know that you can make your environment more conducive to peace, as the work I have done at my mother's home by the airport here in Stonington I hope can attest to. I know that it has brought me many hours of contentment watching her property evolve.

And so this day has brought me full circle, to the greatest gift I ever gave myself – the choice of living my life the way I choose, not having it dictated to me by a culture that has gone money mad. Independent thinkers like myself will always be criticized for our lifestyle, but it is my life – a fact that I discovered on a four-year horseback trip. And to those critics I will disclose a truth I discovered along my travels: the people most judgmental of others are the ones who are most disenchanted with their own lives.

Don't be afraid to step outside of the crowd, for you will be amazed at what you will find.

DC Vision and Louise

Chapter 7
Through Russia On A Mustang
by
Thomas Stevens

I am not in the habit of handing out the term "intrepid adventurer."
Most people who claim it don't deserve it and most people who deserve it don't usually bother to claim it. If Thomas Stevens were alive today, I would urge him to accept that title and more.

Stevens scouted for the famous African explorer, Henry Morton Stanley, in East Africa. Then in 1886 the American proceeded to pedal a penny-farthing bicycle around the world, seeing the sights in Europe, out racing mobs in Persia, and baffling the Japanese in Yokohama. Nothing was able to delay his triumphant arrival back in San Francisco four years later.

No sooner had he returned to the United States than Stevens was hired by the New York World newspaper to go to Russia on a special assignment. Only this time Stevens was ordered to travel through the heart of the Czar's vast domain on horseback.

Upon arriving in Moscow, Stevens chanced to meet Doc Carver, who billed himself as "the most celebrated champion shot of the Wild West." The American showman was traveling throughout Europe with his troupe of cowboys, Indians, and most importantly, horses.

Stevens managed to buy "Texas, a Hungarian mustang, and a good cowboy saddle made in Houston," from the flamboyant frontier dramatist, before setting off across the vast Russian steppes. As luck would have it, the bicyclist turned equestrian traveler was just in time to meet one of the most famous long distance riders of the late 19th century.

The day was a holiday in the village of Tchudovo.

We were seated on a rude bench, talking to the starosta (mayor), on the afternoon of May 28, 1890. Although it was neither saint's day nor Sunday, the peasants were arrayed in every bit of cheap finery they possessed.

This holiday was special. Sotniac Paishkoff, centurion, or captain of 100 Cossacks, who started May 7, 1889, on one of the most remarkable horseback rides that had ever been made, was coming to the tiny village. The greatest feat of this kind heretofore known to the Russians was that of a military officer a few years earlier, from Moscow to Paris, on which ride however, two horses were used. Paishkoff's ride was from the town of Amoor, on the Pacific ocean, to St. Petersburg. The distance is more than seven thousand versts, or about five thousand miles, and the trip was made on one horse.

Orders had therefore been sent from St. Petersburg, during the latter part of Paishkoff's journey, to have every attention shown to him, and police escorts provided day to day. A small convoy of Cossacks, from the "Czarevitch's Own" Cossack regiment, were dispatched to escort him in to St. Petersburg, a four days' ride away, where a whole regiment was to meet him outside the capital. He was to be promoted and to receive an order and a pension.

Paishkoff was expected to pass through Tchudovo that evening. The street was gay with colors, in which the red shirts of the moujiks (peasants) predominated. A red calico shirt, black velvet trousers, and kneeboots, constitute the moujik's ideal costume. The whole population of the village was streaming leisurely in one direction. Fifty or more small boys were marshaled in a troop and, under the direction of the school-master, marched in very good step, singing lustily as they tramped, after the manner of Russian soldiers.

A deputation of old men came up to where we were sitting and proposed to the mayor that, for the honor of the village, he should proceed along the road at the head of the people to meet and welcome Paishkoff.

"Nay, nay brothers," demurred the starosta, "when the Cossack comes I will have the samovar ready with tea; but from Novgorod to Tchudovo is a long ride, and perhaps he will not arrive before tomorrow morning."

The starosta was right in his surmises. The Cossack rider didn't appear that evening. We passed the night in a moujik's house, and early next morning hired our host to drive us out on the Novgorod road to meet the famous rider.

We met the popular hero a few miles out, and turning back, kept pace with him back to Tchudovo. With him were the escort from the Czarevitch's regiment, an infantry officer from Vladimir, a rural mounted policeman, and a couple of Russian newspaper correspondents.

Paishkoff turned out to be a small, wiry man, twenty-seven years old, with a pleasant face of almost mahogany darkness from the long exposure to the dry, wintry winds of Siberia. He wore the Cossack lambs-wool hat, leather jacket and trousers, with a broad yellow stripe down the latter, and heavy jack boots. He was armed with a British bull-dog revolver and a small sword.

His horse was a big-barreled, stocky gray pony, about fourteen hands high, the exact counterpart of horses one sees in the bronco herds of Wyoming and Colorado. The horse was well chosen for his task. He was all barrel, hams and shoulders. His neck and head seemed scarcely to be parts of the same horse. His pace was a fast ambling walk that carried him over the ground at five miles an hour and left the big chargers of the Czarevitch's Cossacks far to the rear. The escort had to trot occasionally to catch up. This gallant little gray was as sleek and well-conditioned however as if he had just come out of a clover pasture.

Paishkoff raised his cap in reply to our salutation, and when my companion said that I was from America, lifted it again.

"We belong almost to the same part of the world," said he, smiling, "only the sea is between us. We have both traveled a long way, you by ship and train, I on horseback."

Yet the Cossack officer, though pleasant, was inclined to be rather taciturn, and I talked more with the newspaper men than I did with him, calling upon him occasionally for confirmation. One of the reporters was Sergie Riskin, from the Moscow "Listok"; the other was the Novgorod correspondent of the St. Petersburg "Novosti." The latter gentleman handed me a card, on which his name and profession were set forth modestly as follows :

"Neil Ivanovitch Bogdanoffsky, correspondent Northern Telegraph Agency, of the gazette "Novosti" and of the Society of Russian Dramatic Authors and Operatic Composers, Novgorod. Own house and own horse."

The last item of Mr. Bogdanoffsky's identity meant that he lived in his own house and rode his own horse; that is to say, he was a free lance as distinct from Mr. Sergie Riskin and kindred members of the profession, who are employees at a few rubles a month and a house to live in, and who, when called upon to undertake a horse journey, have to ride a hired animal or one belonging to the newspaper.

Mr. Riskin did most of the talking.

Alluding to the Cossack's taciturnity: "Paishkoff is a man of deeds," said he, "rather than words. He is small in stature, yet bigger than all the Cossacks of his escort put together."

Riskin had accompanied the Cossack from Nijni-Novgorod, sending daily reports of his progress to the "Listok." Whether a man of deeds himself, he was most decidedly a man of words. He was jolly, yet in despair. His newspaper, he said, had given him 1,500 rubles to cover expenses from Nijni-Novgorod to St. Petersburg, where, for the honor and glory of his paper, he was expected to drive out in grand style to meet Paishkoff as he neared the end of his ride, and make a lavish display of the "Listok's" wealth and enthusiasm.

Sergie Riskin rattled on, pausing very reluctantly and only for an instant now and then, to enable my companion and interpreter to ask a question. His nervous tension, and his effort to talk faster than the movements of his lips could frame his words and sentences, was almost painful. Paishkoff, he informed us, was a remarkable man in many ways. While he, his comrade of the "Novosti," and almost everybody else he had ever met, drank vodka, the Cossack officer refused to drink anything stronger than kwass, a kind of weak beer made from rye bread.

"At Novgorod," said Mr. Riskin, "there was a grand service of prayer before a celebrated icon in honor of Paishkoff's safe arrival, and after the prayers came a jollification, when the officers, the priests, and all of us got drunk and happy – all but Paishkoff. He would drink nothing but kwass and tea; Paishkoff's a wonderful man. He eats what he likes, just like other people. He wears undergarments of mineral wool; over a linen shirt, which he gets washed every two weeks. During the winter he wore a cholera-belt to protect his stomach from the cold, over a leathern suit. He rises at five in the morning, pops a lump of sugar in his mouth, and drinks tea with lemon in it before starting.

"A few days after starting he was caught in a blizzard and got lost. He was nearly frozen to death, and would never have pulled through but for his horse's intelligence. He gave the horse the rein, and although it was pitch dark and the air was full of blinding snow, the animal found his way back to the last station. Paishkoff rode alone as far as Tomsk, from which point he has been assisted by the police. His only sickness has been a touch of influenza. He had experienced forty degrees of frost (about fifty below zero), but thinks winter the best time to travel in Siberia; the roads are then hard and good, and the cold stimulates the horse to travel. He had met no adventures beyond the blizzard. Wolves ? – he hasn't seen a wolf, and he has never fired his revolver. He has promised to give me his notes and I'm going to write a book about his journey."

We turned from the versatile representative of the Moscow "Listok" to the hero of the ride.

"Sotniac," said my companion, "Mr. Stevens wants to send word about you to America. Tell us the motive of your great journey. Is it to decide a bet ?"

"No, no," replied Paishkoff, "only an Englishman or an American would do such a thing for a bet. My object was to prove the great powers of endurance possessed by the horses of the Amoor."

"How much will you take for your horse when you get to St. Petersburg ?" I asked.

"Money again," returned the Cossack reproachfully, "it would be a sin to exchange this horse for money, after what he has done. All the money in America wouldn't induce me to sell him. He will be taken care of for the rest of his life – pensioned off."

"And you ? – you, too, will be pensioned, I suppose."

"We shall know better about that at St. Petersburg."

As we neared Tchudovo, the whole population of the village was assembled at the entrance to the broad, long street. A beggar rushed up to the Cossack's horse and flung himself on the ground before it, as if begging its rider to trample him under his hoofs. Paishkoff tossed him a coin without halting, and the pony swerved meekly to avoid stepping on the man.

The women crossed themselves and men and boys removed their hats. The old moujiks gave the cue and three hearty cheers went up for the bold "Kazak" as he rode past. Paishkoff acknowledged the honor by holding his hand to his forehead. The eyes of the Cossack escort from the Czarevitch's regiment roamed wolfishly over the picturesque gathering of village damsels, turning in their saddles to prolong their scrutiny as the crowd followed behind. The school-master and his brigade of small urchins tramped solidly in ranks, four deep singing loudly.

The starosta, true to his idea of remaining at his post and extending the hospitality of his samovar, invited Paishkoff and his escort to dismount at his house. They refused to halt, however, and the commanding officer of the Cossacks paid the mayor scant courtesy, as though rebuking him for not coming out to welcome them as the others had done.

I later learned that the reporters sent word to their newspapers that an American had met Paishkoff and offered him 30,000 rubles for his pony, for the purpose of taking it to America to exhibit.

That little item of interest was spread all over Russia !

This is an excerpt from "Through Russia on a Mustang" by Thomas Stevens.

Thomas Stevens and Texas

Chapter 8
Jungle Assault
by
Sharon Muir Watson

When Sharon Muir Watson set off in 1989 with her friend, Ken Roberts, to ride the length of Australia's Bicentennial National Trail, nether of them realized their journey would require them to cross more than 5,000 kilometres of some of the worst horse country on the face of the planet. The two year trek savaged equipment, broke down horses and pushed the two equestrian explorers to the edge of physical exhaustion. But just when things looked really grim, Watson discovered that they can always get worse for a horsewoman riding across an uncharted jungle in the Australian outback.

The horses stamped their feet impatiently, and I shifted my weight in the saddle, unsuccessfully trying to find a dry spot under the dripping canopy of leaves. Ken had been gone for over an hour and I was beginning to worry.

"You won't get through to Mossman on the CREB track after Stewart's Creek," we'd been warned at Daintree the day before. They were right. We'd surveyed the track under the powerlines from the creek crossing the night before. It was steep, slippery, overgrown with giant bracken fern and bamboo vines and nobody had been through in the last ten years. The long bitumen detour around the range was an unsavoury alternative so we'd pressed on to look for another route through the hills we'd been told about.

The horses lifted their miserable, bedraggled heads in unison, interrupting my thoughts. Hearing the faint strains of a cheerful whistle, I caught sight of Ken carefully picking his way down hill through the dim rain-misted forest.

"The good news," said my companion as he came within earshot, "is there's no stinging tree. The bad news is its pretty steep in parts so we'll have to lead the horses on foot. It'll be difficult; but it's not impossible."

It wasn't the trail we'd been looking for, but Ken had found some old blaze marks on trees where surveyors had cut a line through the scrub many years ago. He went ahead to clear a path through the vines while I led Shatah in the lead, hoping the other horses would follow.

They didn't.

Horses peeled off at right angles, preferring to follow the contour rather than climb. Even more cunning, Blaze dropped to the tail, turned around and headed back from where we'd come from.

"Hang on !" I called out to Ken. I went back for Blaze while he rounded up the others.

"We might have to hold on to them," I puffed, returning with my packhorse from the bottom of the hill.

It was only possible to travel the horses in single file and leading two horses each in this manner was awkward. Continually shuffling lead ropes around trees, we had to be careful not to pull the horses down on top of us.

Merlin broke loose from Ken's grasp, skidded downhill, and crashed through the timber until a thicket of sturdy saplings halted his descent. Ken followed closely behind, seizing the lead rope and wrapping it firmly around a tree before his packhorse slid further. Abandoning our system of leading two horses at once, we tried shifting them in stages. We'd come to a grassy patch where the sun would have shown through had it not been raining. Starting up the slope with Shatah, I bogged in the mud and he overtook me and disappeared in the shrubbery above.

Ken scrambled to the top of the pinch and I sent Merlin up next. He laboured under the packs, struggling to hold his footing as Shatah had chopped up the mud and it offered no traction. Ken slid down to assist him.

"Watch out behind you," I screamed, as Shatah appeared out of the vegetation and came slipping and sliding down the mud scree. Ken ducked under Merlin's neck, but his foot stuck in the mud and the grey pony skated over Ken's shin on the way past. Shatah careened into Bob, so I dived on his lead rope and tied him up before he went any further. Ken had managed to pull Merlin to the top where he tied him to a sapling.

I sent Bob next, but he scrambled up beyond Ken's reach, knocking Merlin off his feet on the way past. The sapling to which he was tied bowed over and the knot slipped towards the tip, leaving poor Merlin hanging by his chin. As Ken rushed to his aid, Bob's head and shoulders appeared above.

"Look out," I cried. For the second time that afternoon, Ken flew out to one side as a horse crashed over the top of him. Catching Bob, I tied him up to let him catch his breath and sent Shatah off again. The valiant little pony struggled up through the deepening quagmire. Ken caught him at the top and tied him beside Merlin.

Feeling something irritating on the back of my neck, I scraped the skin with my fingers, opening my palm to reveal a partly engorged leech flip-flopping around in a pool of blood. I shrieked, hurled the slimy creature back into the jungle, lost my balance and fell face-first into the mud. Ken laughed himself silly while I stomped off to get the next horse.

When I led Blaze to the foot of the pinch, my packhorse took one look at the daunting hill and threw himself down in the mud. I dived to one side as his flying hooves sailed past, watching in terror as he hurtled downhill in a sickening cartwheel. A thicket of timber checked his fall, and he wedged upside-down between two sturdy saplings.

Ken and I raced down beside him. We needn't have hurried. Blaze didn't plan on going anywhere! Quite content to stay where he landed, the pack horse lay happily on his back, all four legs in the air, my camera case and crushed duffel bag acting as a cushion underneath.

"Never in my life have I come across a horse as lazy as this one !" announced Ken, standing with his hands on his hips and shaking his head in amazement. "He just took one look at that hill and decided he wouldn't have a bit of it."

Ken hauled the loafing packhorse to his feet and marched him back up the hill. At exactly the same spot, Blaze did his lolly and wound up on his back in the scrub once again. He lay there and sulked, refusing to budge. After pulling off the packs and saddle, Ken picked up a hunk of wood and walloped the lounging horse on the rump. The rotting timber disintegrated on impact, having no effect whatsoever.

It took a solid five minutes of yelling, slapping and heaving to coax the sullen animal to his feet. Dragging and shoving him back up the hill Ken had a brainwave.

"We're not thinking straight," he motioned, smacking the heel of his palm against his forehead. "All we have to do is send Bob up first and bonehead will follow!"

Ken climbed the slope and I sent Bob to him. Blaze nearly mowed me down in his effort to climb up after his mate.

"That mongrel bloody horse climbed up there with no effort whatsoever !" he cursed. "And now we're the poor silly bastards who've gotta hoist his bloody gear up there !"

Shouldering each item, we carried it up piece by piece. With one hand balancing the load on our shoulders and the other digging fingers deep into the mud to gain purchase, it took three trips to cart Blaze's load to the top.

If nothing else, I lost my fear of leeches. Instead of picking them off individually, I waited till there was a whole clump on my neck and swiped them off by the handful.

The next stage was even steeper than the last, taking us a couple of hours to reach a timbered ridge line where the horses had solid ground under their hooves again. We switched back to leading two horses each and made far easier progress until Shatah put his foot down a hole and launched himself towards the edge of the narrow ridge. Ken let go of Merlin and heaved on Shatah's lead rope, spinning him around to crash into Merlin. The impact sent both horses sliding front legs over the slippery track on their haunches, heading for the edge again.

Pouncing on Merlin's lead rope, Ken braced himself to take the strain, but the combined weight of both horses was too great. Ken's feet were pulled out from under him and he landed heavily on his backside. He hung grimly on to the ropes, and it was my turn to laugh as the two horses towed him downhill on the seat of his pants.

Ken's weight acted as a brake-log and the horses slowed down enough to gain their feet. Still unaccustomed to balancing himself under a load, Merlin stumbled over the side of the ridge. He disappeared from view and we scuttled down after him in the fading daylight, dreading what we might find.

Merlin had slid about 10 meters and come to rest in a dog-like sitting position. He'd turned side on to the hill, but the near side pack pushed him away from it and the off side bag hung downhill like dead weight. Only 5 meters away the slope disappeared over the edge of a vertical drop.

"We'll have to offload him, and quickly," Ken assessed. "I don't know how much longer he can hold himself there!" The helpless horse glanced at us, wide-eyed with fright.

"Steady boy," soothed Ken, crawling over above him. He reached down under the front of the uphill pack bag, his fingers groping for the surcingle buckle.

"Bugger it!" he cursed. "I buckled the bloody surcingle up on the wrong side this morning."

Scrambling down with his head level with the bottom of the horse's belly, Ken kneeled on his left leg and straightened his right leg below him as a brace. Placing one hand on Merlin's stomach, he gently pulled the surcingle strap out from the buckle and gave it a tug.

"Holy Hell !" he whispered when the slightest pressure pulled Merlin down towards him.

"Easy boy, easy." Ken thrust both hands against the horse's belly, using himself as a prop. Merlin came to a halt.

Bracing himself again, Ken gave a heftier tug on the surcingle strap, managing to undo the buckle as the pair slipped another six inches closer to the edge of the drop-off. The pack bags and bedroll were deftly cast aside while Ken coaxed the exhausted horse shakily up to the ridge top.

Shock had drained Merlin's energy, so we recovered the bags and bedroll on foot and stacked them on the edge of the pad alongside Blaze's load before continuing.

What a relief when we finally made it out under the powerlines. We tied our horses up and I looked around for somewhere to lie down. Every muscle and limb in my body ached, and all I wanted to do was collapse onto a sodden clump of ferns and go to sleep.

"If you stop now, " said Ken, seeing my intentions, "you'll never get going again. We've still got half a night's work ahead of us. We'll have to bring up all that gear, fish out the tent, bedroll, dry clothes and something to eat, otherwise you'll get pneumonia from lyin' out in the rain all night."

He was right of course. I urged my exhausted body back into the pitch black jungle. Reaching our stack of gear, we picked up a bag each and headed back uphill. I lost count of how many trips it took to lug, drag and wrestle the remaining gear to the top. My dulled senses were only vaguely aware of the agony of my tortured body parts.

"You'll have to set your tent up, because I don't know how to put it together," Ken apologized as we rummaged through pack bags looking for necessary items.

The tent was a tricky little two-man tunnel affair, guaranteed by the manufacturer to outlast a blizzard on Mount Everest. These features weren't much value in the tropics, but I could set up my familiar, nylon fortress with my eyes closed and it was one hundred percent waterproof. Ken's bedroll was soaked right through.

We unrolled his soggy bedroll on the floor of the tent for a mattress and laid my heavy swag canvas on top.

"Yuck, what's this all over my feet?" I exclaimed, discovering a sticky mess when I pulled off my boots.

Ken shone the torch over, illuminating my blood-soaked socks. I shrieked in horror, wondering what damage had befallen my numb, waterlogged feet.

"It's alright, it's only from the leeches," Ken laughed.

The insidious blood-suckers had found their way inside my boots, squeezed through the fabric of my socks and had a good feed on me. After which, their engorged bodies had been crushed to death and the stomach contents absorbed by my socks. Everything about leeches was revolting!

Changing into dry clothes, we huddled inside the tent, opened a tin of spaghetti and ate it straight from the can. There was no chance of getting a fire going tonight so our dehydrated food which needed to be reconstituted in boiling water was of no value.

We'd outstretched a tarp and managed to catch some rain water, but it tasted like muddy canvas. Even the horses turned their noses up at it. The ground was so saturated and muddy that the saddles would have ended up waterlogged if we'd taken them off. We left them on the horses to keep their backs dry, tying them to trees as there was nothing to eat that wasn't poisonous.

In the morning I consulted the map and calculated the distance we'd travelled. From the base of the hill where we'd started our climb to our campsite was barely 800 meters. And it had taken over eight hours.

What a slog it had been! Never, ever in my life before had I felt so exhausted, terrified and uncomfortable as I had been yesterday. Yet it suddenly occurred to me that I'd not once thought of throwing in the towel. There had been nothing to stop me turning around, abandoning Ken and heading for the nearest airport and a ticket back to my comfortable job in a comfortable office. I'd given up on much less demanding tasks in the past. Was I really a masochist, or could it be that I was actually enjoying myself? The memory of Blaze upside down in the mud and Ken tearing his hair out in frustration, brought tears of laughter to my eyes. It HAD been fun! I'd set out to achieve something and battled against all odds to come up trumps.

What's more, horses had taken on more purpose in my life. I dearly loved horses, but I'd never felt as close to them before as I did now. And Ken? How could I abandon him? In little over a week we'd formed such a strong bond of friendship that I couldn't bear the thought of leaving him. I certainly wouldn't let him or the horses down. We were all in this together: We were not individuals, but a team.

This is an excerpt from "The Colour of Courage" by Sharon Muir Watson. It is published by The Long Riders' Guild Press.
Readers in Australia can buy it from Muir Publications.   Their website is http://www.users.bigpond.com/muirpub/mid.htm.

Sharon Muir Watson and Easton

Chapter 9
Blizzard and Blindness
by
Donald Brown

The author of this story, Donald Brown, was, as Voltaire put it, "A perfect Englishman - travelling without motive." He believed that a journey on horse-back was the most absorbing and eventful way to travel, a way to discover the world that becomes a mode of life.

As 1950 came to a close, Brown and his Danish friend, Gorm Skifter, set off to ride their Doler horses, Musti and Pilkis, from a tiny village high in the Arctic Circle, down the length of Norway. The six month journey would have been noteworthy enough, except that Brown decided they should undertake their travels during the arctic winter, "because to go to the North except in the winter seems scarcely sporting, like netting salmon."

While dodging snow storms and lodging with Laplanders, the two horsemen struggled to survive the perils encountered on their historic equestrian journey across the snow-encrusted "Vidda," the frozen northern region of Norway.

Soon after starting on our way again a dark speck grew upon the horizon and at last moved slowly towards us. Then it broke into segments and we saw it for a reindeer caravan, long and plodding. There were perhaps a dozen sledges in single file, each reindeer tied to the back of the sledge in front. Upon the first a Lap sat motionless. Both parties halted, while our guide Per spoke with the leader. Here Gorm had to rely upon Per's interpretation, just as I had to rely upon Gorm for interpretation from Swedish into English. Our Lappish was limited to the greeting, "Bouris, bouris," that is accompanied by an arm upon the other's shoulders. This is magic with a Lapp, warming his face, for it is an age-old welcome on the Vidda, of men sharing solitude and possible peril.

Gorm and I found interest enough in the reindeer. They surprised us by their small size. My ideas, at least, of reindeer had been formed when I was a small boy by the exaggerations of Christmas placards of Santa Claus outside department stores. On the average they are slightly higher than a Shetland pony and no heavier. Frail in appearance, they are quick and enduring and pull a sledge thirty miles in a day on an armful of sage-coloured moss and then sleep contentedly in the frozen snow and sixty degrees of frost.

The thought came to me that just as the snow and sand deserts have their similarities, so have their inhabitants: there is this dependence on their herds, and their nomadism with its seasonal migrations to better grazing, its frequent tents, its tribal system, its hardiness and fatalism, its common sense mixed with superstition, and a love of colour as relief from the usual monotone of their land.

As we parted from the Lapps they drew their caravan off the track to let us pass. My mare seemed unused to reindeer and certainly had no liking for them, for as I led her past she frisked and reared, twisting around me while I held tightly to her bit-ring. And when I mounted she stood rigid with curiosity till I dug in heels and urged her forward

I do not like discolouring the world by looking through tinted glass so I often carried my glasses in my pocket. Today the sun's glare had sharpened and the snow became a blinding ubiquity of light so that I screwed up my eyes against it till they began to ache and a sudden pain struck across my head. I let the reins fall and pulled the glasses from my pocket; but the headache stayed with me for the day as a warning.

Our destination that evening was a Lapp dwelling standing squat and solid in the snow, its heavy unpainted logs interlocked at the corners in the Finnmark fashion. The walls inside were of the same natural logs but decorated here and there by the brightly painted cupboards and Lapp clothing hanging from nails. Reindeer steaks and ceaseless mugs of coffee brewed in a kettle on the black stove were lavished upon a rugged table. The Lapp tried hard but without success to understand why we should travel on horseback rather than reindeer sledge.

We were regarded as a man would be who rode a yak round Piccadilly Circus. No one, he told Pir, had ever ridden across the Vidda in winter and showed us its folly by telling us of three men who rode into the Vidda: two were exhausted by a blizzard and died, while the third tied himself to his horse which brought him unconscious back to Bossekop. But our host offered a practical hint by recalling how in one of the historical sagas a blizzard bound traveler had saved himself by slitting open his horse from throat down to chest and crawling feet first into the warm carcass, from time to time cutting pieces from it to sustain him. This seemed about the most repulsive tale I had ever heard; but if a man were faced with this or death by freezing, which would he choose? I do not know and hope I never shall.

Next morning the intense cold of the past two days had gone; instead there was a mildness in the air and Gorm's thermometer read only fourteen degrees of frost so that we loosened the scarves from around our necks and stuffed our gloves into our pockets. But our Lapp guide Per looked about the horizon without content. Some people are never satisfied, we thought and went on in the beneficence of the sun.

But we had been barely an hour upon the trail when there came a slow greying of the sky along the horizon to the east, creeping upon the sun. While the grey ate away the blue, a movement in the air began to break up the stillness and blow the dry snow about the horses' feet, lightly lifting their manes and rippling their tales.

The sun was dimmed and at last put out and a coldness struck down at us, prompting us to again wrap our scarves around our necks. Frozen flakes which had drifted low like sand blown along the sea-shore began to rise with the wind and swirl about the horses' heads and then ours and above us we knew not how far.

Now the temperature which had gone down steadily since the coming of the cloud suddenly dropped as if the bottom had fallen from it. The silver line on the thermometer withdrew its bulb like a snail to its shell as the wind wailed up to a gale. It was reading 63 degrees of frost (100 plus degrees below freezing)   and still it fell. We dismounted and went beside the horses to ease the numbness of our bodies, bending our heads and almost shutting our eyes against the flogging of the blizzard. We half covered our faces with our scarves till our breath froze upon them and stuck them to the skin. We pulled them painfully from us. Then the snow crystals blew into my beard and set solid upon my jowl. Certainly there was little comfort today upon the Vidda.

We were a silent company; once or twice we tried to speak cheerfully but the cold went down our throats and strangled speech so that the only communication was by insistent search from near-closed eyes for dark movements, an outline of a man and a horse, or a sledge and a horse's straining shoulders. We went together in a cell walled by swirling snow; today we did not wish to go alone, for that would not be freedom but confinement. At intervals a gaunt pole or a doubled-up and quivering branch loomed wailing into our cell, passed by us and faded out behind.

There was no thought today of lunch, only a resolve to come out of this blizzard; no one thought, there was only numbed feeling: the feeling of your face set hard as in cement and now anesthetized by cold against the stinging of the storm; the palsy of your arms, one set stiff as a cripple's, the other crooked tensely round your reins. Only your legs felt the pulse of blood; powered by the will they thrust forward heavily.

We went slowly and laboriously, for as polar explorers have testified, the battering of a blizzard exhausts both mind and body in a strange and insidious way. If a man comes to the limit of his endurance (which is probably more mental than physical) he will give way to the irresistible desire for sleep and lie down in the snow. But it is a sleep from which he will not awake.

In the afternoon we came to what we feared to find – places where there was no longer a trail, the ruts filled in and smoothed out by drifting snow. At first it was a few feet, then yards, and I wondered whether we should have to dig-in and how we could shelter the horses. By standing the sledge on its side and buttressing it with the tea-chests perhaps but this would be poor shelter.

Several times the one in the lead paused to bend down and look for the trail; once or twice we could not find it and went on in hopeful search.

But at last towards evening the blizzard seemed to weaken. At first we dared not hope lest it be a pause to gather greater force but now we went upright where before we had leant upon the storm and the white wall had gone back from us; so when a pale light filtered down from the sun we turned one to the other in relief that cracked the frozen skin around the eyes. Soon the sun came down brightly and thawed out the stiffness from our bodies; the snow blew about aimlessly for a while before settling lightly upon the ground. The blizzard was over.

At evening the trail came out upon a long and frozen lake. The sun was already falling from us, washing the shelving eastern shores in gold. As we rode, separately now because speech was discord, lake and low hills changed subtly to rose and to red and deep cold-blue shadows reached out longer across the lake. An early moon big as a dinner-plate stood against the sky upon the ledge of the horizon. The stillness had crept back behind the storm and there was no sound in the world but a soft rhythmic crunch of snow beneath the horses' hooves.

As we rounded the bend of the shore, a caravan of reindeer sledges trailed towards us, led silently by Lapps. The white and the blue, the red and the yellow of them were the snow and the shadows and the radiant hills; the cold crisp tinkle of the reindeer bells was ice. Man was playing in harmony with Nature, point and counterpoint. As we passed, no one spoke; only were there grave liftings of hands, for this was not the time for hearty greetings. Now I thought I understood why the Lapps are nomads and that I knew the reason for their peaceful minds.

Gradually the lake narrowed to a river that sank slowly between its banks and all was ever-deepening blue and once again the cold cut sharply through our furs. At last, as we came round the bending bank, it uncovered lights one by one and revealed Kautokeino, that lonely settlement in the snow.

The street ran sparkling beneath lights that dimmed the windows of dwellings to a mellow amber. Now and then a door remote from the street opened to silhouette for a moment a bulbous figure black upon yellow.

And then down a slope of the track there slid a sleigh along the soundless snow, drawn by a tall dashing reindeer flaunting his antlers high. A Lapp upon the sleigh, gay in scarlet and yellow and blue, crouched forward from his furs to flick the reindeer with his whip. And as they went by a sleigh bell tinkled. It seemed unreal, like a stage scene from a pantomime beneath its brilliant lights; it was Fairyland and Santa Claus. I cannot say that he drives his reindeer over roof-tops or drops down chimneys, for these we never saw, but no one can tell me there is no Santa Claus.

This is an excerpt from "Journey from the Arctic" by Donald Brown.

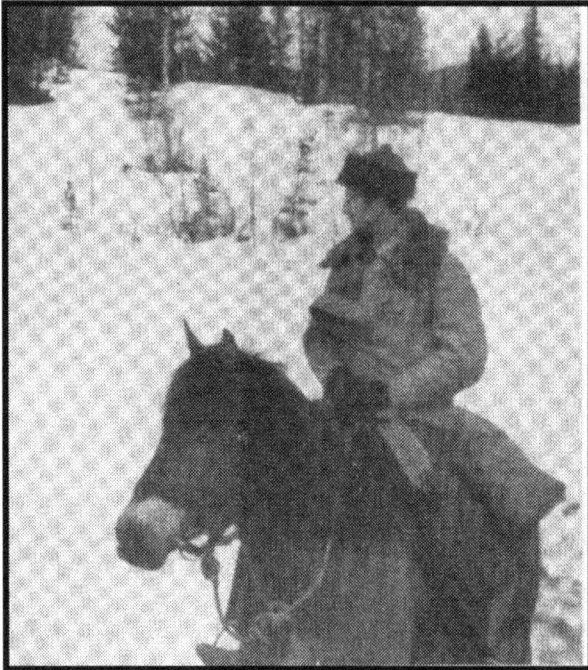

Donald Brown and Musti

Chapter 10
Forgotten Heroes
By
Darcy Morger-Grovenstein

Who were the heroes of the 20ᵗʰ Century? Were they the creators of the auto-mobile and airplane? Perhaps they were inventors of computers, space rockets, and medicines. In truth, real heroes were also little-known men with an amazing vision and hearts as big as the American country they rode across. Of this heroic saga there are four: brothers George and Charles Beck, Jay Ransom, and Raymond Rayne.

In 1912 to 1915, these men, known as the "Overland Westerners," completed the longest equestrian ride of the century. Well documented, somehow their accomplishments have gone unrecognized outside of the equestrian world. There are no stories in Ripley's Believe It or Not, and the Guinness Book of World Records has not included this feat. The years have served injustice to these heroes. This story is a reminder of their astonishing journey.

A horse logger on the Olympic Peninsular, George Beck was well into his life at 36 when he decided taking a turn in the saddle was better than wielding an ax. The lumber business was slow and George talked his younger brother, Charles Beck, into taking a little horse ride around the country via all state capitols in the 48 states. The length of this "little ride" would be 20,352 plus miles (almost the equivalent of a span around the Earth). Though not entirely enthusiastic, Charles had recently been laid off from the railroad, and George convinced him that this would be the horse ride of the century.

Together the brothers from Bainbridge Island, Washington approached another family member, their brother-in-law, J. B. "Jay" Ransom. Also known as "Slim," Jay was intrigued with the thought that perhaps a three-year ride around the U.S. might bring better financial pickings for his young family and definitely more fame than the life of logging. He thought the trio of horsemen should round out to a nice quartet by adding one Raymond "Fat" Rayne. The fourth partner in this tour was anything but fat, a skinny sprite of but 20 years: "Fat" was hankering for adventure, fame, and the ultimate chance to be a cowboy. "Slim" and "Fat" hailed from the town of Shelton, Washington, the official starting point of the ride. To this day, the town of Shelton calls these Overland Westerners "their boys." The age of automobiles or "horseless carriages" was rapidly overtaking the days when a good horse was the most reliable mode of transportation.

George was the quixotic leader of the group. He proposed the idea to friends with the explanation that logging right then was a lousy business with up to six months of downtime a year. He pointed out that the World's Fair, The Panama Pacific International Exposition, was going to be held in San Francisco in 1915. The justification for such a trip as theirs lay in the "gold" they were sure to reap at the end of their famous ride. "We have the nags and gear," Beck stated, "Let's make the longest horse ride on record and get ourselves a reputation. We'll win fame. We'll write an adventure book. We'll put on a show on the midway at the Exposition. There's a pot of gold out there and we'll find it!"

The plan: Officially begin in Shelton, Washington on May 1, 1912. Ride by horseback to all 48 state capitols starting in Olympia, Washington on May 1, 1912 all the way to Sacramento, California in May of 1915. They would finish the ride in San Francisco on June 1, 1915 just in time for its opening of the World's Fair: The Panama Pacific International Exposition. A diligent course would taken them into the southern states during the two upcoming winters and yet deliver them on time "to be the toast of the World's Fair." The route mapped out by Beck bore dots of the state capitols connected by lines forming a hopeful constellation on paper.

As a promotional maneuver, the forthcoming achievement of the Overland Westerners would verify the quality of horse breeding in the Pacific Northwest. Their advertised intent was the completion of the entire trip by one or more of their horses. The poster hailed this enterprise by stating: "This will accomplish the greatest traveling feat ever known in the history of horse flesh – in considera-tion of the changes of climate, feed and water, the conditions of the barns and roads, and the hardships of a ride of this nature."

The men hoped to finance the estimated $9,000 needed for trip expenses such as food, horse feed, tack, film, printing costs, and incidentals, by selling printed keepsakes such as 5 cent postcards and fifteen cent poster/calendars. The calendars included the years 1912 – 1915 along with portraits of the Overland Westerners, a map of their planned route, and photographs of "Pinto," the horse they counted on completing the route. They would carry with them print masters to re-up their supply of printed material as needed. To supplement selling souvenirs, George agreed to sell subscriptions to a small Seattle magazine called The Westerner in exchange for half of the one-dollar subscription. The Westerner agreed to act as sponsor for the group and would promote the historic ride by covering the progress of the trip. (However, any prospect of corporate underwriting withered when this magazine folded in the few months after the Overland Westerners began their trek.)

Included at the beginning of the trip were horses for each of the men, and the Morab packhorse named Pinto. At 900 lbs. and fifteen hands high, the six-year-old paint bred of Morgan and Arabian stock soon became George's own saddle horse.

On May 1, 1912, the Overland Westerners left Shelton, Washington for their first official visit to a state capitol, Olympia, Washington, which lay only 18 miles to the south. It was there they were received by Governor Hay and given a template for a "Certificate of Call" documenting their arrival as well as a letter of introduction to Oregon's Governor West. At the end of their journey three years later the quartet had 48 state verification documents from state governors authenticating their expedition.

However balmy their departure from friends, family and well wishers gathered at the capitol building, they soon realized their goal would not be easily met. Only a few miles out of Olympia they began encountering the first of their countless challenges. Wet, muddy roads over the Pacific Highway proved grueling for the new adventures. By the end of the first day they and their horses were exhausted.

As the men learned to pace themselves in the saddle they continued to head south. On this route to Oregon's capitol in Salem, the Overland Westerners picked up the last official team member. He was an enthusiastic Gordon/Newfoundland puppy named "Nip" and from that day on he acted as one of the crew. Nip's enthusiasm was contagious as the men greeted their second governor and cheerfully headed out on the next leg of their mission.

But summer had not yet come to the high country. May 23rd found the four riding east over the Cascade Mountains. Here the passes were still covered with seven-foot snowdrifts. They spent a night in a deserted cabin, half-freezing and exhausted. Setting out to cross the summit in early morning, George wrote of the attempt: "Got to the snowline at 5 a.m. and then the fun began, although it was better than we anticipated having frozen some the night before. It held us up pretty well. But the horses went through to their belly once in a while. It tired them out pretty much on the start as it was pretty tough work and new to them. But when they got their second wind they done better and somewhat steadier. I thought once we would never make her but a fellow can do more than he thinks he can if he makes up his mind and we made up our minds to go through or bust."

The Overland Westerners did make it through and went on to conquer the miles filled in with the whole gamut of experience, from downright tedium to bursts of fun and contentment. In Idaho they involved themselves in a baseball game between two rival mining camps. Riding out to the site took five hours by buckboard. Fat Rayne umpired the lively game on a field they had to first clear of sagebrush. Lasting until well after dark, they counted their blessings of a good supper that night that "did not cost a cent." At the Idaho state capitol of Boise, George as invited to ride Pinto, the Morab, in the traveling 101 Wild West show.

Montana was remembered fondly by the Westerners, as they liked the folks who greeted them hospitably and knew enough of horse riding to appreciate the effects that hard riding could make on a rider or horse. Farmers and ranchers provided meals, shelter, and grazing pasture free of charge as they traversed the broad expanse of the state's 700 miles that summer. In Helena, they were warmly welcomed by Governor Norris. George remarked that night in his journal, "We found Governor Norris to be a prince, and also his secretary. We also got introduced to Edgar S. Paxson, the famous cowboy artist who was doing some work in the new wing of the Capitol building at the time. We also saw one of Russell's famous paintings and went all through the capitol building, and she certainly is a fine one."

It was in Helena that the character and reputation of the team was tested. While the group was in town routinely soliciting their posters and postcards, Fat's saddle was stolen. The men approached saddle maker, Fred J. Nye, for a replacement bridle and saddle for $54. This was a huge monetary gouge for the men who were already struggling financially to keep up with purchasing new horses for worn out ones. George Beck was emphatic in leaving collateral – their tent, camera, and rifle – until the debt could be paid. Beck stated, "We are gentle-men tourists on horseback with a self-appointed mission. We are not saddle bums."

The foursome endured every kind of pestilence and hardship along the way. From awful storms to searing heat, the Overland Westerners kept steady on their mark toward their goal, averaging 22 miles a day. The insects proved the most vexing. Horseflies, mosquitoes and of course "critters" became constant irritants. En route to Bozeman from Helena, the men were caught in a midsummer storm. Beck wrote, "We no more than got our things off the horses than she started to come down. Thundered and lightened something fierce. We put our things in an old log house nearby and found shelter for the night, although it was full of rats and bugs. We tore the paper of the walls to lie on the floor, as they were certainly very dirty. 'Slim' was awakened several times with the rats nibbling at his hair, but any kind of lay-out on such a night was welcomed."

Like any long and arduous expedition, the party had several brushes with tra-gedy that could have abruptly ended their quest. Trouble presented itself again the day the men reached the Powder River in south-eastern Montana. The stalwart Morab, Pinto, was almost drowned. You can hear the tension in Beck's journal recollection: "We had forded dozens of busy rivers. Jay tested the stream with a long pole, and then rode over to show us how it could be done. Everything went find until he got in midstream when Pinto carrying our pack, which slipped, flipped over and couldn't flip back. I thought he was a gone horse, but Jay hung on, flipped him over right side up, and headed him upstream and snaked him to shallow water.... We lost some grub and a few utensils but we were very glad to escape that easy by saving Pinto."

The riders continued east. The miles and hours in the saddle became both adventure and burden. Discomfort and hunger were often the norm, yet the Westerners kept their sights on their mission and the easy times success would bring. Through all their trials they remained true and honest cowboys. The little profit made from selling postcards and posters went to providing for their horses first. Nip fended for himself and sometimes the four men with an occasional catch of rabbit. They all looked to the elder Beck brother, George, as the captain of the team and guardian of the animals. "Fat" Rayne respected George as an honorable stockman. He told the Denver Post, "That man [George Beck] surely knows and loves horses, and cares for them too. We could be choked with thirst, empty-bellied, ready to pitch on our dumb heads from the saddle with weariness, but the broncs came first. They were fed, rubbed down and blanketed and, if necessary, put under cover. Only then did we rustle for our own eats and shelter."

One year turned into the next and then the next as the Westerners crisscrossed the continent. The routine of canvassing the souvenirs, greeting politicians, and changing road-worn horses wearied the men as one state after another came and went. Not only did the men grow hard and lean, but they also became excellent riders. As they worked their way back west with but a few thousand miles to go, a rancher in Wyoming offered free horses to the four if they could ride them. Confidently George recalled, "We could ride 'em. You learn how to ride, no matter which way they twist, after you have forked a hayburner a few thousand miles."

The thought of the finish line drove them hard that spring of 1915. They pushed themselves to meet their deadline in San Francisco, California for the opening of the World's Fair. They arrived exactly on schedule, 20,352 miles lay spent since the day they left home three years and one month before. They had gone through seventeen horses and yet Pinto, as predicted, completed the entire course. Nip had also been through it all except for the first bit he missed. The men had spent exactly the estimated $9,000 between them. They had traveled a record of 1,127 days without serious injury to themselves or their horses. Now only fame and wealth could be ahead for them.

But the events of the trip's conclusion were anything but profitable. No one greeted them as they rode into their celebration of the opening of the Panama Canal. In fact, a cop yelled at them to "get them hayburners off the street!" The lively crowd was more interested in the belly dancer, "Little Sheba," than four bone-weary equestrian heroes.

Their story and historic accomplishment was soon lost to a world on the brink of World War I. Pushed aside at the Exposition, fair-goers focused on the development of the automobile, a model of the Grand Canyon, and the reproduction of the Panama Canal. The weary Overland Westerners had not reserved a concession booth for the promotion of their story and the selling of their wares and none was found available. It was no satisfaction for them to know that the World's Fair itself was also proving a "flop."

Movie producer Rex Beach and writer Jack London turned down George's ideas for an adventure book or movie. George recalled, "The pot of gold we had been pursuing had moved out, way out into the Pacific ocean by the time we reached San Francisco." George stayed on a while in California hoping to eke out some interest for their tale, while the other three sold what they could and hopped a freight train heading for Washington state.

Eventually, George was able to save up enough for fares on a tramp steamer for himself, Pinto, and Nip. The downtrodden troupe of heroes returned home with little but memories intact. George tried unsuccessfully again and again to write a narrative of their heroic expedition. He said, "I wrote it sweet enough but it came up sour."

The Overland Westerners set a goal and completed the longest equestrian ride of the 20th Century! Where is the historic recognition for such an incredible journey? Where are the national accolades for accomplishing this record-breaking feat? Little is known of these visionary and dedicated men. They settled back into difficult remainders of ordinary lives. George drowned drunk in a roadside ditch on Bainbridge Island. Nip soon followed in death. Pinto was tragically sent to the nearby Olympia National Forest to serve as a packhorse on the dank and dreary trails. The magnificent Morab, a true equine hero, lived out his life there. Forgotten were the glory days of his epic journey.

In 1920, Frank Heath, a fervent horseman, retraced a portion of the route of the Overland Westerners just eight years after their journey. He found no monuments or accolades to mark their ride. Circumstances of unfortunate timing had rendered the Overland Westerners as forgotten and uncelebrated.

It may take time to recognize our heroes in history, to laud the dreamers and the riders of the dream. There is no question that time has sifted through the conquests of similar missions, to discover that the Overland Westerners really did deserve the fame. George Beck had said it: "This will accomplish the greatest traveling feat known in the history of horse flesh."

And they did it. Heroes all. Perhaps now they know it.

This article, originally entitled "The Overland Westerners – Unsung American Heroes," first appeared in the April, 2003 issue of "Trail Blazer" magazine. It appears in this anthology courtesy of the author, Darcy Morger-Grovenstein and Trail Blazer's publisher, Susan Gibson.

Charles Beck and Bill, Dick and Jay Ransom, Ladd and Raymond Rayne, Pinto, George Beck and Blaze.

Chapter 11
Winter Sketches From The Saddle
by
John Codman

Few equestrian travelers can claim the additional distinction of being an equine philosopher. Yet John Codman, the self-acclaimed " septuagenarian" author of this tale, was never shy about sharing his horse based opinions. A life long traveler, Codman preferred to avoid carriages, citing his belief that, "it is not safe to take risks at my age so I stick to the saddle." Besides, he tells his readers, "there is no greater pleasure in locomotion than to find myself on the outside of a horse."

Throughout the pages of his rare book he not only weaves in his own heartfelt equestrian philosophy, but regales the reader with his wintertime exploits. Along with his mare, Fanny, the 70-plus-year-old rambler undertakes a ride through the snow-covered landscape of old New England during the winter of 1887.

There are two modes of healthful locomotion left to us, pedestrianism and horseback exercise. I make no account of the unnatural bicycle, which doctors tell us is productive of serious disorders when used to excess. Walking is a solitary entertainment. It has no variety in its measured steps, although it is valuable for its economy when time is not considered. But there is the companionship of the horse, and the change of gait bringing many muscles into play, which gives a peculiar zest to riding.

I have thus developed a favorite medical system, which I shall style Equestrianopathy. It is vastly superior to Allopathy, Homeopathy, Electropathy or pathy of any other kind.

"When pain and anguish wring the brow," whether it comes from mental or physical depression, too much exercise of brain or stomach, dissipation of society or confinement in furnace-heated hotels or offices of the city, I resort to my remedy.

From my boyhood I have adopted it whenever opportunity offered, as a prophylactic as well as a cure. Many hundreds of miles have I ridden over African deserts, South American pampas and the plains and mountains of California, Utah and Idaho; and the miles traversed in New York and New England might be counted by thousands. But for the horse I should have long ago been in the grave.

"My kingdom for a horse !" exclaimed King Richard. The horse has been a kingdom for me.

I could say with Campbell :

"Cease every joy to glimmer on my mind.

But leave, oh leave the light of hope behind," that hope being by saddle horse.

The late Rev. Dr. Cutler of Brooklyn, when a feeble young man, recovered his health by riding from Portland, Maine to Savannah, Georgia. His valuable life was prolonged to old age by this almost daily exercise. When one of his parishioners asked how he could afford to keep a horse, Cutler's reply was, "My dear sir, I cannot afford not to keep one."

If your business confines you to the city, give the night two hours that you steal from it, and take from the day two hours that you give to sleep. Take this clear gain of time for horseback exercise in the park. But if you are a man of leisure, ride through the country for days and weeks on long journeys, where constantly recurring changes divert the mind that stagnates in daily routine.

Procure – I mean buy, own an animal that is exclusively a saddle horse. A horse is like a servant in one especial respect. A servant of all work is perfect for nothing. She is a poor cook, a poor parlor-girl and a poor chamber-maid. A horse that goes double and single in harness and is likewise used under a saddle, walks, trots and lopes indifferently. A good driving and riding horse is a rare combination, and a horse generally used under harness is never capable of any prolonged journey under the saddle.

Select a horse whose weight corresponds in proportion to your own. He should be a fast walker, a good trotter and an easy loper. A fast walk is the quality most desirable, though not often sufficiently considered. Walk your horse half the time and divide the other half between a trot and a lope. Now as to the saddle. The little "pig skin" is adapted to hunting and is well enough for play and exercise in the park. It is used by exquisites who ape all things English.

Did you ever notice that such persons carry a Malacca riding crop with a rectangular ivory or steel handle, with a loop at the other end of the stick ? Ask them the use of it and they will tell you it is the fashion. Really it is useful to country gentlemen of England, who, riding where lanes and gates abound, are enabled, without dismounting, to catch the gate latch, and to close the gate after them with the handle. They also put a lash into the loop when hunting, but such a thing is an encumbrance here.

The English saddle is not well adapted to long journeys. It often galls the horse's back, which the unstuffed Mexican or McClellan never does, if properly put far enough aft and with a blanket underneath.

Especially is this true in regard to a lady's saddle. If a horse could speak he would tell you which he likes best. I wish that Balaam's ass when he was in a conversational mood, had said something definite on the subject of saddles. Be kind, while you are firm with your horse. Don't carry a whip – he will see it and suspect you. Wear light spurs, which are good persuasives and which he will think have touched him accidentally, while at the same time they serve to keep him awake.

Loosen the girths frequently when you alight, and when you stop for any time remove the saddle and wash his back. The beast will thank you with grateful eyes.

Do not give him water when hot, excepting enough to wet his mouth. Feed him when cool, but feed neither him nor yourself immediately before starting, nor when greatly fatigued. The neglect of this precaution may induce dyspepsia for a horse as well as a man.

Don't trust the most honest face in the world in the matter of oats. See them put into the manger, and hang about the stable until your horse is fed. Feed your horse with four quarts of oats in the morning, two at noon and six at night, with all the hay he cares to eat.

Get your own dinner afterwards, for you are of less importance. If your table is not properly served you can complain. Your horse cannot. Do not overload him with too much baggage. Dead weight tells upon him more than live weight. Dismount occasionally when about to descend a long or steep hill. You thus relieve the horse and vary the exercise of your own muscles. Wear a woolen shirt and let him carry your night-shirt, hair-brush, tooth-brush, bathing sponge, a few shirt collars and handkerchiefs; they will weigh but little over two pounds and will be all sufficient.

In summer the rapid motion of riding prevents a concentration of the sun's rays, but it is in the winter that it starts the blood into circulation, and if the nose becomes red, the cheeks are red also and the glow of health pervades the whole body. With proper precautions, the rider needs not suffer from the cold even in the severest weather.

I cannot call to remembrance the novel, but it is one of Scott's, where the hero is about to start for the Highlands in the company of an old farmer, who, carefully wraps the steel stirrups with straw for the purpose of keeping the rider's feet warm. I have always remembered that hint, and have found the practice to be effectual.

Avoid at all times, on foot and on horseback, especially on horseback, the unhealthful India-rubber boot or shoe. They are inventions of the undertaker. If you would keep your feet warm and dry, put on thick-soled boots of thick, upper leathers too, not by any means tight, and wear thin cotton socks with woolen socks over them, and when riding in very cold weather, felt overshoes over the boots. These are not in general use, and I have had some difficulty in obtaining them. In response to numerous inquiries, the shoe-dealers told that they had not this article. At last a facetious shopkeeper said that he had plenty of felt slippers, and that he had one pair made for a Chicago girl which were not big enough for her, but he thought they might go over my boots. They did. So much for stirrups and boots.

To change to the head. Put your soft felt hat in your pocket. Wear a toboggan cap, which may be pulled down over your ears, and over your nose if need be. Wear a cardigan jacket, and button your pea-jacket tightly around your neck. Carry a stable blanket in this wise, remembering that you are to use a McClellan saddle, as I counseled you to do not so long ago; double the blanket, and, leaving just enough to go under the saddle, allow the most of it to fall over the horse's neck till you are mounted. Having mounted, pull the remainder of it over your legs, and start, for now you are ready. You may face snowstorms and blizzards, and you will actually enjoy them as I did.

As I am unable to persuade any human friend to accompany me on my long rides, my companionship with my mount, Fanny, becomes closer. Fanny knows the pocket in which I keep the little lumps of sugar. When she gets one of these little dainties, she acknowledges it by a cordial shake of hoof and head. She knows perfectly well whether we are about to take a long or short journey, for in the first case I always show her the small roll of baggage before it is buckled upon the saddle. So she adapts her gait to the requirements of the trip.

We talk together along the road – that is to say, I talk to her and she listens, many people think this is the best way to carry on a conversation. It is not uncommon, and it always affords pleasure to one person at least. By this means the rider may place himself "en rapport" with his horse. There is no English for this French term. It means a great deal – not precisely that a man is part of a horse, or that a horse is any part of a man, but that the man for the time is equine, and the horse is human in his feelings.

To the saying of Terence that because he was a man nothing was foreign to him, I would add that for the same reason nothing about a horse can be foreign to me. I believe that a horse has a soul. The Bible tells us that there are horses in heaven, and that they came down from thence to take up Elijah. I think that even bad men get to heaven at last, and there is no reason why horses, who are better than they are, should not get there before them. Several years ago this question of immortality of animals was discussed in the columns of the New York "Evening Post." It was shown that many men of sound mind believed in it – prophets and apostles of old, like Isaiah and John the Revelator; later theologians, like Martin Luther, and scientists like Cuvier and Agassiz.

It was very cold on the morning of the 16th of February. The mercury at eight o'clock stood at five degrees below zero, but the air was perfectly still, so that at ten, when the glass indicated zero, the lack of wind aided by the sun-warmth already appreciable in the advance of the season, rendered riding not only far from uncomfortable, but gave it a zest and enjoyment not to be attained under any other condition.

Leaving Lake Mohegan we pursued our noiseless way over the well-beaten sleigh tracks, down through the village of Peeksgill, meeting here and there a muffled pedestrian. To all appearances a great field lay before us. Why should Fanny suppose it to be anything else? She had never been there before. Why should she know that beneath that fair covering of snow there was a layer of ice, and that beneath the ice was the Hudson River, and enough water to drown a thousand regiments of cavalry. There was not the slightest difference in the look of the snow upon the river and the land over which we came to it.

Nevertheless, she was so reluctant to follow the foot tracks that I was obliged to dismount and give her a "stern warning." Even then, when once upon the river, she trembled excessively, and looking into her eye I could see the thought in her little brain, and knew that if she could speak she would say, "I have every confidence in you, but I am a female and you must make allowances for me. You say the ice is two feet thick; but I might break in. Can't we go around by the bridge at Albany or the ferry in New York city ? No ? 'Come on Fanny, is it?' That's all well enough for you. You say you will lead me till I gain more confidence; but these are the tracks of men. Horses weigh a great deal more than men, and I don't see a single horsetrack on the snow !"

Caresses and sugar, however, had some effect, but she stepped timidly and gingerly along until we came to the well-marked sleigh track. All at once her fears vanished as she trod it with a firm step, and permitting me to mount her, she loped over the frozen river as if it had been a highway upon the land. Animal instinct, was it ? No; it was thought, reflection, calculation, like that of a man, without his knowledge of safety – nervousness, fear, distrust, like that of a woman, who refuses to be overcome by reason.

So we went on confidently and satisfactorily until suddenly there came one of those, to the inexperienced, fearful ice-quakes, giving the impression that our weight was cracking and breaking down the great winter-bridge through all its length and breadth, and that we were about to sink into the depths below. The hills on either side took up the echo, and poor Fanny thought that her last moment had come, and that she was about to expire in a convulsion of nature.

She stood still and trembled from head to foot. Cold as it was, the sweat broke out upon her, and with it the hair on her skin literally stood on end. I never so pitied a dumb thinking beast.

Dismounting, I put my arm around her neck, drew her head to my breast, patted her face, and kissed her check, yes, I did, and I walked by her side comforting her as best I could for the rest of the way, as again and again the fearful, though harmless, crashes reverberated from shore to shore. For her sake, I was glad when we landed at Haverstraw.

This is an excerpt from "Winter Sketches from the Saddle" by John Codman.

John Codman and Fanny

Chapter 12
Through Persia On A Sidesaddle
by
Ella Sykes

In a time when polite Victorian society severely curtailed a woman's activities, the author of this story risked her life daily. Religious fanatics failed to frighten her. Forsaken, hostile deserts never slowed her horse bound progress. Instead she rode side saddle 2,000 miles across Persia, a country few other European woman had ever travelled through, accompanied by her Swiss maid, older brother, and 50 camels loaded with china, crystal, linens, and fine wine.

Her name was Ella Sykes and in her day she was accounted one of the bravest women alive. Today her remarkable story, replete with rajas and rogues, camels and caravans, is long forgotten.

She broke the rules in 1894 when she agreed to accompany her older brother, Captain Molesworth Sykes, on a diplomatic mission to the ancient city of Kerman, Persia. His job was to further the interests of the British Raj. Ella's was to run the household for her bachelor brother and avoid being assassinated by Moslem fanatics who found her very presence an insult. During the next two years, the Sykes siblings lived cut off from the rest of the world, the sole European occupants of a city where the only thing more hostile than the natives was the environment.

Despite a host of hardships, Ella thrived on the life of adventure she discovered in Persia. Like her brother, she spent every spare moment in the saddle. Yet unlike her more comfortably clad companion, Ella's Victorian principles did not allow her to discard either her heavy, riding habit or side-saddle, a combination which proved nearly lethal on more than one occasion. The following excerpts reflect both her skill as an extraordinary horsewoman and her endurance as a pioneer equestrian explorer. Though she described herself as simply, "Miss Sykes, an unmarried young woman," the indomitable Ella was a great deal more!

The Journey to Kerman, Persia

It appears to me that the East either powerfully attracts or as powerfully repels those who have left the West for the first time. Most real travellers, however, succumb to a charm which is somewhat difficult to describe, as it is the mixture of many things that makes up the undoubted fascination of the whole. Probably there is a spice of the nomad in every one, and, if so, Persia is the very land to call it forth. There is a great sense of freedom in travelling week after week across vast plains, where often the only sign of life is the withered scrub which at night will do duty for firewood, the traveler ever pressing forwards to some range of superbly coloured hills which must be surmounted in the future.

Day after day the sun's rays shine down from a deep-blue heaven, in which there is seldom a cloud, and pierce through an atmosphere so pure that every seam and fissure in peaks, several miles off, may be clearly distinguished. The air blows free and untainted across the deserts, an air so fresh and exhilarating, that it feels almost like champagne in the blood, warding off fatigue, and endowing the wayfarer with such vigour that he is enabled to enjoy everything thoroughly, taking the bad along with the good.

The shackles of civilization are left behind. There are no trains or steamboats to be caught, no crowded hotels to stop at. The traveler leaves one guest-house after another without regret; camp after camp is pitched and then struck, inducing a constant eagerness to press on and reach the next stage of the march. And yet there is no hurry about it all. The caravan halts at the pleasure of its master, and stops as long as he chooses, the tent-life making the journey one delightful picnic.

And the charm of the life is increased tenfold to those who love horses, and who travel, as we did, with their own animals. In the East the horse becomes a friend. It will often follow its master like a dog, will wander about camp un-picketed, strolling up to beg for a bit of bread or sugar, and is, in short, such a comrade that the traveler gets into the habit of spending all odds and ends of time in the congenial occupation of "looking after the horses." Usually his last thought at night is to see if they are comfortably wrapped up in their thick felts, and his step is the signal for a low neighing for his equine friends, those lying down not attempting to get up, so confident are they of his good intentions.

Then, again, the great solitude of Persia strikes the imagination. Days may pass without coming across a village or meeting an inhabitant. Man seems indeed a small thing, as the caravan slowly crawls over some vast plain always encircled by peaks, flushed with many a shade of madder or mauve, standing up, sharply silhouetted against the intense blue of the great cloudless vault above them. Such a complete contrast to the bustle and hurry of the West – a contrast between lands, in one of which time is money and in the other of no account at all – forces the mind to view everything from a new standpoint. Civilization appears to fall away here, and man is brought back to the simple facts of humanity, and has an uneasy sense that up to now his life has been sadly unreal and artificial. He feels that a broader, truer glimpse of existence is being vouchsafed to him, and as he mingles with a people whose standpoint of morals and manners is an entirely different one to his, he learns not to judge from appearances, and the precept of "live and let live" becomes deeply engraved on his soul.

And through it all, with each fresh experience, the sense of a glad freedom is interwoven. The traveller knows that joy in living, a joy which our civilization has done its best to improve away. Pessimism is unknown here, morbid thoughts cannot exist, and life is better, because so much happier. Perhaps, however, I have not really hit upon what constitutes the glamour of the East. My love of it may be partly owing to the novelty of my experiences, partly to a longing for travel and adventure never satisfied hitherto, and, it is possible, chiefly to the fact that I had never been so happy in all my life before.

On Leaving Persia

However, the feeling of depression did not last long when once we were fairly started on our journey of six hundred miles to the frontier. And perhaps what distracted my thoughts more than anything else was the fact that I was riding a new horse for the first time – a horse that had never had a lady on its back before, or a sidesaddle and an English bridle; and to me there are few things more interesting than to get the mastery over a spirited animal, and to establish that delightful sympathy which makes the rider and his steed as one.

So hurrah for the road again !

Hurrah for nomadic existence !

And hurrah for the wanderlust that lurks in each man's blood, and drives our English race so far from home and kindred over the face of the globe !

The Journey Back to England

On February 1st, 1897, we said goodbye to Teheran for the last time; but now we were going home instead of turning our faces to the wilds as before. We galloped out with some of our friends a couple of miles beyond the Kasvin Gate. One or two people said they thought the sky looked uncommonly as if it were working up for snow, but the day, though cold and windy, was bright and the muleteers assured us that all the winter's snow had fallen, and that the early Persian spring was at hand.

However at Kasvin we soon came to a region of deep slush, the melting snow on either side draining down into the road. My steed had an unpleasant tendency to topple over on its head, and needed energetic urgings on my part to get it along the twelve miles to the mud village of Agha Baba, where we halted and lunched before attempting the seven miles on to Masrah.

The whole country was now covered with thick snow, which had only partially thawed in this high region, and we were obliged to ride at a foot's pace in single file, along a narrow track which abounded with holes filled with muddy water. Our poor horses tripped and stumbled in a pitiable way, every now and again breaking through a thin crust of frozen snow, and plunging down into deep holes, making their riders feel far from comfortable. A few caravans of heavily laden mules met us lumbering along, and there was then much danger of a collision, as one party or the other was obliged to leave the track and plunge into the deep snow at the side. We noticed with some anxiety, that the sky was covered with grey clouds and had a steely blue line on the horizon; but our guide was positive that it would not snow; nevertheless, fine flakes began to descend as we picked our way down to the village of Masrah, dirty and tumbled-down, with its guest house in ruins.

We knew that a heavy snow fall would probably block the Kharzan Pass over the Elbruz Range, which was the critical portion of our journey, and neither Molesworth nor I relished a lengthy sojourn in two small rooms, reported to be infested with the poisonous bugs for which Masrah is notorious. We started off therefore at 7:30 a.m. to do the worst part of our ride. Our horses stepped briskly in single file along a narrow track, beaten down on the crisp, frozen snow, and we felt that at this rate the ride would be a mere bagatelle.

Ahead of us were some fifty or sixty mules and donkeys, toiling laboriously along, making the path, and when we came up with them we naturally wished to pass; the wind being so cold that it pierced our wraps as if they had been made merely of paper. However, it was easier to talk about getting in front of these caravans than to do it.

We tried to force our way past a line of humble donkeys, which swerved off the track into the deep snow lying on either side, and straightway fell over, loads and all. Then we attempted to struggle through the snow ourselves, and in a moment our horses were floundering, helplessly, their legs slipping from under them and we slipping off their saddles. However there was nothing for it but to persevere, and we remounted our steeds, which plunged a second time up to their shoulders, while we again fell off. So we resolved to lead them, and managed to walk in tolerable comfort on the fairly hard snow past the caravans, our ponies struggling after us as best they could. We now found that we were, in a way, the pioneers of the road, the snow lying smooth and untrodden ahead of us, covering a series of low hills rising one above the other to the crest of the pass. There was, of course, no track of any kind; but we mounted and went straight upwards, the snow getting deeper as we proceeded, and our unfortunate horses rolling us and themselves more frequently.

At last we were obliged to take to our legs again, and the next two or three hours will be forever engraved on my memory. The sun was rapidly melting the snow, therefore we could not walk on its upper crust, as we were able to do at first, but sank at each step up to our knees, and occasionally much further if we were unlucky enough to get into a drift. What with the labour of such walking, the rarefied atmosphere, and the intense cold, I frankly confess that I could have sat down and wept from sheer exhaustion. I did my best to follow in my brother's footsteps, but it was weary work pulling oneself up from hole after hole, and our progress was painfully slow and fatiguing.

Everything, however, has an end sooner or later, and when we had achieved our fifth undulation it dawned upon us that the snow was less deep, so we took heart and remounted, seeing some way off the village of Kharzan and a great caravan approaching us. We crawled carefully down the next hill, our guide Sultan Sukru and his horse turning a complete somersault on the way; and then came the problem of how we were to pass the slowly moving mule caravan, as there was only room for one animal on the track at a time.

My brother, who was leading, struck out into the deep snow, and his horse and a mule from the caravan rolled over together, so, that he had some difficulty getting clear of their hoofs, and hardly had he recovered himself than my steed sat down on me, and I judged it wiser to slide off. With many a tumble and struggle we managed to pass the long string of mules and reach the beaten track again, after which we proceeded merrily to Kharzan, having taken five hours to do six miles, but being too thankful to have accomplished it to complain of the difficulties of the route.

The next day we made a late start about 8:30 a.m. and as rain was falling we decided to ride straight on instead of making a mid-day halt of lunch. It was a good thing we did not tarry, for half-way we encountered a mild form of blizzard, the rain coming down like a waterspout, while hailstones were driven into our faces by such violent gusts of wind that our horses swerved from them again and again. My waterproof cape was soaked through, and nearly torn from my back by the fury of the tempest, I was almost blinded with the hail, and if my brother had not lashed at my steed with his hunting-whip I scarcely know how I should have ridden the reluctant creature along the road, which now seemed interminable. It was indeed a relief to reach the guest house at the village of Menjil and find a fire by which to warm ourselves, for we were literally wet through, and had to wait three hours before our caravan arrived with dry clothing.

Next day we had to negotiate a long thirty miles to Resht in order to catch our steamer, which left on the following mid-day, and as it had frozen during the night we found the roads in a terrible condition.

After a while we came to the forest, and here the Russian Road Company was at work, pulling up the old cobbled causeway, which, with all its deficiencies was certainly preferable to the sea of liquid mud left in its stead. Through this our unfortunate ponies waded, nearly toppling on their heads, and my heart was often in my mouth as we escaped again and again almost as if by a miracle, from being rolled over into the foot-deep mire. The caravans of small donkeys we passed were coated with mud from head to foot, and in one place a camel, left by its owner, was placidly lying down in a mud bath, evidently considering death a lesser evil than further struggles through such rivers of slush.

We reached the village of Kuhdum about mid-day, but no carriages were in waiting to drive us onto the port, owing to the state of the road, and after a halt for lunch we strapped the baggage we intended to take with us to England on the backs of three horses, and set off at a rough jog-trot, riding behind the loaded animals to keep them up to the mark.

The roads were truly execrable, the mud often reaching to our horses' knees as we hurried painfully along; and every now and then a box got unloosened, and rolling off ignominiously into the mire, had to be fished out and fastened on afresh.

Molesworth and I reached the outskirts of Resht at sunset. It seemed as if we should never find the British Consulate through the labyrinth of narrow alleys, and when we arrived it was to find the house locked up and the servants gone, their master being away in Europe. However, one of the soldiers on guard managed to open a window, by which we entered, and then he went to hunt up the servants. The adventures of the day were even then not over, for our wood-fire set the chimney alight, and the servants in trying to extinguish it, made a hole in the roof, the general excitement delaying the arrival of our dinner to an unpleasantly late hour.

We made our way to England from Constantinople via Vienna and Paris, reaching home in March 1897, and had the joy of meeting relatives and friends, and of feeling that it was good to return to our own country again.

But in spite of my pleasure at being at home, it is difficult to realize that I have, in all probability, left the East forever; and as I wake up morning after morning to the soft greys and greens and blues of an English landscape, I miss the glow of the floods of golden sunshine that were wont to pour into my room in Persia, and often close my eyes again to imagine that I am back once more in that well-loved country.

Only in my fancy am I in Persia again, feeling a boundless energy and strength with which to carry out the duties of the day lying in front of me. Once again I am on the march, and we are eating a hasty breakfast in the chilly, starlit darkness before sunrise, while the tents are being struck and the groaning camels loaded up. I can feel the freshness of the morning air, as, huddled in our cloaks, we walk along, leading our horses, and watching the daily marvel of the dawn, where the sun seems indeed to spring into the heavens as a giant refreshed. Then later we mount our steeds, and perhaps ride across some great, dun-coloured plain towards a range of brilliant-tinted mountains, a ride through an utterly barren, desolate country which yet possessed an enchantment that held me from the first to the very last.

The cheerful tinkle of the caravan, the gleam of white tents, rambles in the cool evenings, and dreamless nights are among my reminiscences, coupled with the life-giving air, which coursed like wine through my veins and enabled me to laugh at fatigue and discomfort.

This is an excerpt from "Through Persia on a Sidesaddle" by Ella Sykes.

California Coast Trails
by
J. Smeaton Chase

It was 1912 and the age of equestrian travel was coming to a close. Sensing that the world as he knew it was undergoing permanent changes, J. Smeaton Chase set out to ride from El Monte, California, north to the Oregon border. A noted artist, poet, photographer and naturalist, Chase was ever mindful of the beauties of the countryside he proposed to ride through. Thus accompanied by his gelding, Chino, the equestrian poet headed north without itinerary, his only plan and purpose being simply "to take in the country."

The scenes he described, of a rustic Arcadian paradise, peopled with happy peasant farmers, half-forgotten Spanish missions and the abundance of Nature's still untouched beauty, stands in stark contrast to the California that exists today, with its freeways and toiling millions clustered together in vast, concrete mega-cities.

Chase's story details a lost world seen from horseback, a vanished time from the world's youth when a traveling man could smoke his pipe in peace, while contemplating the beauty of God's country from the back of his saddle.

All that day I plodded quietly along, ruminating lazily to the pad, pad, pad of Chino's hoofs. After passing a minute hamlet called Bonsall Bridge, we rested for half an hour beside the road, under a sycamore in the fresh young leaves of which the horse discovered an interesting flavour. These roadside interludes are very pleasant, you tie your horse in the shade, take off the bridle, loosen the cinch, pull out your bread and cheese, and munch to the rustle of leaves and interrogative comments of hidden birds.

The brook purls along, and your thoughts purl along with it. A draught of water, and then the careful packing of the pipe-bowl, and the first grateful puffs. You slip the bridle on, tighten up the girth, swing into the saddle, and ride on with one little vignette added to the many such, of which one is turned up now and then by some chance occurrence; whereupon there comes back to you the whole scene, with your companion, if you had one, or your faithful horse, now perhaps obeying another hand, or none.

While I was lingering near the remains of an old orchard, to give Chino a chance to graze, a cloud of dust and a hilarious whooping told of the approach of a bunch of cattle. They were convoyed by five cowboys in sombreros and chaps, who stopped to fraternize with a brother horseman. They had been four days on their way from the San Luis ranges, and were loud in envy when they learned that I was two months out and still had more than half my journey before me.

Two of them at once offered to "trade jobs" with me, without even waiting to hear the nature of my business. When they understood this they were urgent to accompany me, and thought they might be useful in "working the picture box" or even "doing the poetry stunts."

But, finding that their beef was spreading over too wide a territory while we talked, they suddenly jerked their ponies round and with blithe shouts of "Adios!" jingled away in a whirlwind of dust.

Next morning I continued up the canyon, which is a winding and very beautiful one, shaded with oaks and sycamores of the finest. After a few miles the road leaves the bottom and begins the long climb to the ridge. Just where the ascent commences I found a mountain farm. On the window of the house was painted the proprietor's name and the word "Comidas," signifying "Meals." The place was rustic and inviting, and I tied Chino to the gatepost and entered.

A pleasant Mexican woman with a rollicking baby answered my knock. Certainly she could cook me a meal, but, "Ay, senior! Nothing is there in the house but eggs, with bread and coffee." I wanted nothing better, and seated myself at the table for proof. In a few minutes she returned with my eggs, deliciously cooked in oil that came, I learned, from the olive trees in the hillside orchard. Presently the husband came in. He picked up the baby, Bernardito the Jolly, and they all sat down for a chat while I ate.

They were of middle age, but had only been married a year or two, and it was delightful to see his pride in her and their love and enthusiasm for the baby. His admirable qualities – and he was all admirable – were pointed out carefully to me, and I was charged to report them every one to a compatriot of the husband's who lived in the next county; how strong he was, and how big! his hair, so long for only ten months! his three small teeth with which already he would bite his father's work-hardened finger, behold ! as if he were a little pig, the chica ! And so on, pouring out their simple love in all friendliness. Altogether, I do not know when I have more enjoyed a meal than my dish of eggs at that rough plank table with those good people.

Later Chino and I took our way up the steep slope. The mountain side faced south, and had no shade, and the sun was at its hottest. Not so hot, however, as the desert sun of our previous summer's journey, as I reminded Chino when we halted for a breath. As we climbed, the view opened finely and became constantly more striking. Even in California it would not be easy to match that superb panorama. A foreground of flowery brush fell away steeply into a purple mystery of mountain and canyon, dreaming in the wistful haze of summer: at five miles' distance the infinite plain of sea shone softly under the southern sun; far out the islands of the channel showed like fairy isles, mere shadow shapes of darker tone against the pallid blue of the horizon. Right and left ran the high, wavering crest of the Santa Ynez mountains, with here and there a sentinel pine breaking the ease of the long undulations.

On nearing the summit oaks began to appear, often surrounded with lakelets of tender grass, interesting to Chino. Here I found growing freely the lovely globe-tulip (Calochortus albus), a white saint of a flower, all ethereal gentleness and tranquillity, the purest looking blossom I know. I think a pirate would look at it with reverence. With it grew many other flowering plants, – nemophilias, geraniums, marguerites, brodiaeas, anemones, collinsias, making little floral sanctuaries among the rough and thorny world of the brush.

About the pass the oaks became larger, and among them grew a few beautiful madronos. This great arbustus is one of the most striking of Western trees, handsome in leaf, blossom, and fruit, and especially noticeable for its smooth stem of satiny buff or red bark. Its long, gleaming arms make a gallant appearance amid the sombre olive of oak and pine, and with its tassels of scarlet berries the tree looks well equal to the part of "Captain of the Western Wood," for which Bret Harte nominated it.

While I rested by a spring, eating wild strawberries and noting where the deer had lately left their imprints, four Mexican children came by on their way from school, as they told me. Their temple of learning must be of the smallest, for I had seen no house except one deserted adobe house since I left my lunch place, three hours before.

Crossing the divide, we turned down the northern face of the mountain through a splendid woodland of oak, laurel, madrono and maple. A roaring stream, Ballard Creek, ran in a deep canyon below the road. We marched rapidly down the steep descent. The sun was setting, and pools of solemn shadow crept in among the golden hills, the Lomas de la Purificacion, that opened before me. How beautiful are the Spanish names ! They seem to throw a cloistered quiet, an hermitical calm, over the wide, sunny landscapes. One would think that angels had chosen them.

I found an excellent camping-place on a little bench of land above the stream. The moon was full, with light of that warm, almost orange, colour that one sometimes see in summer. It was late before I could bring myself to turn in, and then I lay for a long time enjoying a moon-bath, and watching the swaying pennons of Spanish moss that hung form the great oak overhead. Chino was tethered in a foot-high growth of clover, and put me to sleep at last with the rhythm of his molars.

This is an excerpt from "California Coast Trails" by J. Smeaton Chase.

J. Smeaton Chase and Chino.

Chapter 14
Eastward Ho ! Into Asia
by
Anna Louise Strong

Few equestrian travelers had a more politically radical life than did the author of this story, the American, Anna Louise Strong. Having been raised in Seattle, Washington in the early 1900's, Strong turned her back on her otherwise normal suburban roots. Denouncing the evils of capitalism, she began a series of state-sponsored journeys deep into the secretive heart of the recently formed Soviet Union. Her resulting books described a worker's paradise and invariably praised the communist experiment. Dictator Joseph Stalin was so pleased with this American convert, he encouraged her to visit the far flung corners of the new Red Empire.

In 1929 Strong was offered the chance of an adventure of a lifetime, to accompany a group of Soviet geologists who were preparing to penetrate into the seldom-seen Pamir mountains of far off Tadjikistan.

This story finds the political free thinker turned equestrian explorer as she attempts to buy a horse in one of the famous Central Asian horse markets.

The headquarters in Osh of the Pamir Expedition of Geologists was a tiny shack, which furnished indoor sleeping place for barely four people. Its chief qualification was the large pasture around it, where a score of horses were feeding. Near a great open shed of a barn which was stacked with much dunnage, Professor Nikitin of Leningrad was engaged in showing some green helpers how to put packs on horses. He came to a pause in the work and led me inside the house to a small room which served as dining room, office and general assembly.

"The trouble with our crowd," he remarked whimsically, "is that we have too many experts and not enough plain workmen. Plus, we should have left yesterday, but there are always delays at the end. We must take with us every spool of thread, every knife, every pin that we shall need till October. When you add to this the fact that we must take large supplies of goods of which there is a shortage in Russia, and must have special permits to secure them, you see that it is not done in a hurry. However, the delay is not serious, for we hear that the trails are still blocked by heavy snows beyond the Alai plateau."

Nitikin's expedition, I learned, was sent out by the Geological Committee to investigate the deposits of precious minerals known to exist in the Pamir mountains. The expedition consisted of thirty persons. Divided into three groups and scattered for a hundred kilometers across trackless peaks and glaciers, these geologists were to toil at an elevation of thirteen thousand feet and upwards till the October snows drove them from the heights.

The first steps towards my journey was clearly to buy a horse. On this all agreed, though the Soviet geologists and army men had different opinions about the price I must give. Commander Lavroff assured me that decent horses were not to be had for under three hundred rubles; he himself had recently bought an excellent steed in Fergana for seven hundred. Professor Nikitin reassured me.

"You are not joining the cavalry," he said smiling. "We bought our mountain nags for one hundred and fifty rubles in Northern Kirghizistan. I will send our workman, Artumov, with you to the market."

I must admit at once that I know nothing of horses. Save for short trips in my childhood on ponies in the Seattle Zoological Gardens, one of which threw me over a hedge, I had never ridden horseback till the previous summer in the Caucasus Mountains. On that occasion, crossing the main ridge through the wilds of Chechnia and Daghistan, I had traveled several hundred miles on seven different nags and saddles, averaging two days on each. On the last three days, our native guides compelled us to ride on the pack saddles, on which they intended to carry freight on the return journey. These wooden frames, padded by my bedding, I admit that I found little worse than other saddles – a confession which completes the display of my ignorance to any experienced horseman.

The weekly horse market at Osh came on the morning of the twenty-second. When I reached the geologist's camp, the two workmen had already gone to the market, and I was told to go after and find them. It was some distance away in the native city. A drive by cab brought me in twenty minutes to a level ground by the river, whence arose the great dust and din of much stamping and chatter. I pressed through a gate in an improvised barrier kept by a guard, and found myself in the horse market of Osh.

Irregularly in every direction horses were tethered – to trees, to stumps, to the ends of wagons. A central space had been cleared, and here a dozen beasts were tramping about, being tried out by prospective owners. There was no barrier between the crowds and the cleared space; horses pushed into the crowd, and the crowd pushed into the horses. To proceed even a few feet forward it was necessary to shove through jostling Kirghiz tribesmen and dive under the heads of horses. More than half an hour I sought in this melee, but found no trace of the Geological Expedition.

By the time I located my cab driver, who was also inspecting horses, and returned to Professor Nikitin, the morning was far advanced. It seemed doubtful whether the horse market would keep open long enough for us to revisit it. But Artumov, the workman, now agreed to return and take the chance with me. We were further delayed by a stop at the post office to draw out some money, for Artumov told me I must take at least three hundred rubles.

"You weigh how much?" asked Artumov bluntly. "One hundred and eighty pounds? And you intend to take no pack horse, but to put your personal baggage also on your riding horse. Say sixty to seventy pounds more – two hundred and fifty in all. This weight the horse must carry day after day over high passes where the air is thin and the grass scanty. Clearly you need a horse of the hills who can work on a grass diet; but clearly, also, he must be a strong beast. These little creatures that sell for less than two hundred rubles would drop under you before you crossed the Pamir mountains.

Artumov clearly knew his business, which was to carry two hundred and fifty pounds of weight securely over the Pamirs. I would trust his judgment, making only one reservation; I would try the horse myself to test his gait. This, after all, was the only point of a horse which I could judge. Artumov warned me that the hour was late, and the market would be thinning. We should have to take, and quickly, the best of what we found.

To my inexperienced eyes there still seemed an endless number of horses, but Artumov pointed out that most were not for sale, or were impossible for my purpose.

"Here is one that might do," he said at last, approaching a placid-looking beast of mixed brown shades. He leaped into the saddle and rode back and forth in the cleared space. "Easy gait," he said. "Suppose you try him."

Of all the seven horses I had ridden in the Caucasus, only one seemed in recollection to have had a gait as easy as this one. Surely on such a horse I should not be unduly tired. The owner wanted three hundred and fifty rubles, so we looked elsewhere, coming back each time to the first one. A Russian peasant speaking Kirghiz thrust himself into the discussion, volunteering to interpret for us. He praised our choice of a horse so fervently that I suspected him of being in league with the owner, till I saw that he praised just as fervently each horse we turned towards.

We decided to begin bargaining. The owner assured us that the horse was well worth three hundred and fifty or even four hundred rubles, but since the market was now nearly over, we might have it for three hundred. Only three hundred; it was a sin not to grab him at once for such a price the owner said. He was in fact insulting his horse to suggest it. Plus the horse was young; he pulled open the mouth and bade us note six years of age.

Artumov nodded; but the horses' mouth meant nothing at all to me. The horse was Kashgar-bred and mountain-trained, the owner said, strong and surefooted. When I asked about his trot, which I had been unable to test in so small a space, the owner replied scornfully that Kashgar horses never trotted; they took the "wide stride," which was nearly as fast as a trot and capable of being kept up indefinitely. I was in an optimistic mood, and "wide stride" sounded much less painful than my memories of Caucasian trotters.

We offered two hundred rubles; the owner protested at our crime. To insult such a horse with two hundred was clearly impossible. Artumov informed him that we were not millionaires and must still buy a saddle. Would he leave an American woman, the guest of his nation, to go without a saddle to the Pamirs because she paid so much for a horse?

The owner assured us that on such a horse the saddle was of little importance. A saddle like that on him now could be bought, with all its gear, for a mere twenty rubles. I suggested that he sell me his saddle for that price, but Artumov refused to translate this. The Mohammadans of the region, he said, never sell a horse and saddle together. Naked the horse was born and naked he must go to his new master. Even the lead rope by which he is taken away must be new.

By degrees his price came down and ours went up till we met at two hundred and fifty rubles.

"I think it is his last word," said Artumov. "Better take it."

Our volunteer peasant interpreter was loud in his assertions that nowhere could we get such a horse for two hundred and fifty rubles. We agreed to buy; and thereupon found that there was still to pay a seven and a half ruble registry fee to the horse market, which should have been included in our bargaining but for our ignorance. The former owner agreed to pay two and a half rubles towards it, leaving me to pay five. A formal paper was given me from the market, stamped and sealed, declaring me the owner.

All that I knew of my acquisition was that his gait was easy; this, in fact, was all I was capable of knowing. I had Artumov's assurance that he was strong and young, which seemed the chief requisite for a Pamir trip. I noticed that my six-year-old was a stallion, and not a mare or a gelding, but that fact at the time would have meant nothing to me. I was later to learn the capricious temper that characterized my new possession, and won him in every caravan the reputation of being "a good horse with a bad character." He had seemed to me even a trifle slow and lazy; he was, until it suited him to be otherwise.

Our self-appointed interpreter refused to leave us; he seemed tireless in his devotion to our interests. He insisted on showing us the saddle shops, but the saddles were all expensive. They were Uzbek models, built of wood, with a small saucer-like seat, and painted in gaudy designs. Predominantly red in color, a saddle and all its trappings cost fifty rubles. Artumov thought that Nikitin had a second-hand saddle he might sell us. We decided to end our shopping, and, by way of dismissing our officious interpreter, we stopped at a chaikhana and offered him some tea.

We were, however, not to get rid of him so easily. It now appeared he was a professional go-between in the market. Praising horses was the way he made his living; he cared not which horse, as long as the sale was made. Two rubles it took to content him; I had no way of knowing what he may have received from the seller.

We returned to Professor Nikitin and readily secured the second-hand saddle for twenty rubles – an Uzbek saucer-shaped saddle.

"The exact shape matters little," said all these travelers. "The saddle is only a base on which to pile saddlebags and bedding. It is the latter you must arrange for comfort."

The professor bade me pack and be ready to leave by noon tomorrow.

As an afterthought he asked me if I had yet secured my G.P.U. (forerunner of the KGB) permit, allowing me to enter the Pamirs. I told him I had a visa from Moscow.

"It is not enough. You must go in the morning to the G.P.U., and get a paper showing that you are registered and giving your expected route."

In some concern I presented myself next morning at the office as soon as it opened.

"Certainly you need a permit," said the official. "Otherwise you would be sent back."

The official signed the necessary permit and gave me the paper which read: "Permit for Citizeness Anna Louise Strong to enter the forbidden frontier zone and to travel in it on the route Osh – Alai – Horog and return, good until August 27, 1929."

As I read this detailed limitation of my journey, I realized how very far beyond the usual routes I was venturing, beyond even the half-forbidden Turkestan into which foreigners penetrate with difficulty. I was to enter the "forbidden frontier zone" for which even Professor Nikitin needed a permit.

There remained an hour before noon in which to pack my baggage. There was not much of it, but the placing of every object must be carefully considered. I had not only to pack it so that I might carry it all on the horse, but also so that the perishable things, like Kodak films, should be guarded against the vicissitudes of the journey, against horse's sweat, and rain, and the splashing of water from forded rivers.

I had bought the day before a pair of saddlebags of native make, as large as I could find and of firmly woven cotton cords. These were in no way waterproof and could not be counted on as protection, only as containers. At the bottom of one bag I placed a single folded bed sheet. Next to the sheet went a small tight roll of summer clothing; three thin dresses, a rayon chemise, and two pair of stockings. Somewhere I might emerge at last in civilization, and these things were for that shabby preparation. In this saddlebag also went reserves: an extra cake of laundry soap, some extra Vaseline, and grease paint against high altitudes.

Into the other saddlebag went my small German rucksack containing one woolen blouse, six batteries for my flashlight wrapped in handkerchiefs, wool socks and two changes of underwear. For such extra warmth I had a thin sweater, a pair of wool breeches, and an ancient wool skirt such as we use in Seattle for mountain camps. Also into this bag went such food supplies as I carried, an army can of beef and a few lepeshka, the hard, round biscuit loaves of Central Asia. I supplemented these hopes with a water canteen, some sugar, dried apricots, coffee, tea and cocoa.

Thus lightly armed I prepared to set forth into the Pamirs. I had not even a coat; my jacket of forestry cloth had been stolen in the Caucasus, and ordinary coats are a burden to the touch in the heat of Central Asia. At the last moment in leaving Moscow, I had taken a Mexican serape, which had hitherto served me only as a sofa ornament. In addition to this was a sleeping bag, made of a comforter of camels' wool bought in Urga, and covered with airplane linen left from Quaker supplies in the days of the Russian famine.

Promptly at noon I reached Nikitin's camp at the town's edge. The first two groups of geologists had set off many days before, followed a few days later by the heavy baggage on camels. There was left a small caravan of nine persons and twenty horses. By the time the horses were half packed it was five o'clock. Storm clouds were gathering, rain seemed imminent. Most of the party began to protest that they should wait till the morrow; was it worth getting wet in order to camp ten miles or so down the road?

This time the genial Professor Nikitin proved obdurate.

"It is worth even a wetting," he said, "to try our packs once and get out of Osh."

We therefore left the town at 6:40 in the evening, a most belated hour for beginning an expedition. Behind the mountain called Suliman's Throne, an angry orange glow spread up the sky, where the storm made sunset appear before the appointed hour. Steadily our road mounted and snow peaks came into view, only to be lost again as we dipped behind nearer hills. It was a wide, rough road beaten by many centuries of caravans. In no way was it steep or difficult. Yet our pack animals fell often, either from bad loading or because they were poor horses. We had not yet learned to adjust the heavier loads to the stronger beasts, or even to tie the loads properly.

Professor Nitikin's irony of having "too many expert geologists and not enough men who can hitch a horse" was clearly true; and the need of a first short evening to "try our packs" was evident,

My horse kept easily along near the head of the procession. I decided to name him, and wavered between "Pamir" and "Alai," each of which seemed appropriate. But since the Pamirs are the graveyard of horses, while the high Alai plateau is the paradise of all live stock, I gave him, in gratitude for his first evening's performance, the pleasanter name.

Yet I learned the rest of the party had already dubbed him "American Girl."

This is an excerpt from "The Road to the Grey Pamir" by Anna Louise Strong.

Chapter 15
My Kingdom For A Horse
by
Margaret Leigh

In the autumn of 1939 a young Englishwoman faced a difficult choice. Margaret Leigh had just sold her farm in Cornwall and wanted to return to her ancestral home in the Highlands of Scotland. Yet how to get there ? The obvious choice would have included either a train or automobile. However Leigh had a strong streak of adventure running through her. She opted for that altar of travel, the saddle, dismissing those nay-sayers who said the deed couldn't be done in such a modern era.

The resulting trip was reminiscent of Goldilocks' remarks about her discoveries in the home of the Three Bears. It was neither too hot, nor too cold, not too long, nor too short. It was in fact, just right !

Though England was rushing headlong into the disaster of the Second World War, Leigh and her mare, Ladybird, passed through unscathed, observing the twilight of a rural lifestyle that had lasted for centuries. Her remarkable book is both poetic and practical. Therefore I have included excerpts which illustrate her progress through one of the loveliest rides of the 20th century.

Why Journey on Horseback ?

I have often been asked if this trek was made for a wager. Hardly: for there is nothing adventurous, nor even very strenuous, in a horseback journey on English roads. In a country so thoroughly mapped, organized, and provisioned, fast traffic is the only danger, and all one needs is plodding patience, and the sense to keep off major roads and away from large towns. With quiet horses, good weather, and reasonably short daily marches, a ride of some weeks' duration is within anyone's compass, though the business of swimming against the stream is often a trial to nerves and tempers.

For riding is a slow, anachronistic mode of travel, and nothing is ready for the horseman, neither stabling, nor corn, nor a decent surface to ride on. He must find his own routes and make his own arrangements as he goes. Everything depends on the good-will of local farmers: but in my own experience there is a widespread interest and sympathy with horses and horsemen. Only once was I refused a night's grazing, and this because the farmer was away and his wife afraid of strangers.

Still more often have I been asked why I was riding from Cornwall to Scotland when it would have been much quicker and easier to go by car or by train. I wanted to learn the technique of long-distance horseback travelling under easy conditions in a civilized country, and then see whether I had sufficient strength and resource to do the same thing in wilder places. For dozens of people have said: "How much I envy you!"

Long distance riding is not all fun, indeed it is often the reverse, but it is well worth trying for a season, and most certainly worth reading about in an armchair, or considering for one of those holidays when tomorrow is never spoilt by becoming today.

Getting Under Way

I began to prepare for the road in September, 1938. Much of my preparatory work was useless; but one learns by experience, and must reckon that of the stuff so carefully made ready, one quarter will be abandoned at the start, and half will be thrown away upon the march. This is true even of important and well-organized expeditions: and when you have strewn your route with useless gadgets, and arrive with nothing but your saddle and waterproof cape, it is comforting to think that better men than you, with more valuable equipment, have done the same thing. The happy traveller, like the successful bridge player, must know what to discard: and the more he discards, the happier he will be. Even if the equipment kept is simple enough, in practice it often seems too much, and the labour of packing and unpacking, and still more of keeping the stuff in tolerable preservation, cannot be believed without trial.

And now a word of warning about military saddles. You see a whole collection of handy-looking dees, and start tying things on with string, until the saddle looks like a stall at a jumble sale. Then having mounted with difficulty, you advance a certain distance, till thumping and rattling noises, increasing with every step, warn you that things are working loose. You proceed a bit further, and the thumping changes to intermittent dull thuds as one thing after another falls to the ground. Without trial, it is hard to realize how quickly the movement of a horse, even at a walk, will slacken the knots of string most firmly tied; and even if the string holds, the package will be gradually disintegrated by the everlasting bumping on the saddle, or worse still, against the horse's warm moist flank.

It is a safe rule to have everything three times as durable as you think necessary. There is no doubt that for real comfort in riding, nothing whatever should be carried on the saddle, and the long-distance rider who travels *deluxe* will have his equipment sent on by car. But this is hardly playing the game.

I have no technical knowledge of horses, but one learns much from experience, and I am sure that the best mount for a long journey is not a hunter or a riding-school hack, but a solid, hardy farm cob or herdsman's pony, with plenty of grit and endurance, easy to catch and quiet in traffic.

In long-distance riding the walk is the pace that counts, and a fast walker, with long smooth stride, is always to be preferred. The pack-horse should be narrow, smooth-paced, and at least as fast as the leader. For a led horse always tends to drag, and if he is a slow walker, the whole troop will be delayed. In theory, all trek horses should be exercised beforehand, on gradually lengthening marches, with the saddles, riders, and loads they are expected to carry.

I never exceeded twenty-five miles a day, and mostly did less. I never travelled on Sunday, and there was no trotting. This kind of travel is, I am sure, less hard on horses that hunting three days a week, or regular ploughing. The chief difficulty is the hardness of the roads, but much may be done by keeping to the by-ways and grass verges, and if your horse has really sound feet, he will not suffer much. As the old groom said, "It's not the 'ackin' nor the 'untin', nor yet the 'oppin' over 'edges as 'urts the 'osses' 'offs, but the 'ammer, 'ammer, 'ammer on the 'ard 'igh road."

And after the horses, the horseman.

"Don't you go," said my old landlord, with great earnestness. "You'll be stiff for life. You won't listen now, but some day you'll remember what I said."

He was too pessimistic. The first week out I was a little stiff and a little sore, but nothing to matter; after that I got hard and could have continued indefinitely. Those who are used to riding need not worry. So much for physical fitness, which is perhaps less important than the right state of mind. The rush of modern life has made us impatient of delay, and most of us find it hard to adapt ourselves to the slow pace of travel on horseback. On English roads there are no thrills, no adventures, hardly any danger, but plenty of petty discomforts and unforeseen checks, which demand an unfailing supply of patience and good temper, with a robust cheerfulness and sense of humour.

Last Minute Regrets

That night I did not sleep very much. The sleeping bag was comfortable, not to say luxurious, but I was filled with that restless excitement and foreboding which makes a journey's eve its most appalling moment. We long for change, for adventure, and when it is near would like to call it off. What madness lead us here, we ask ourselves; could we not even now get out of it?

Cornwall

The glen was no more than a shallow cup in the moor, full of bracken and gorse and the glimmer of granite boulders; and beside the stream were enclosures of grass, cropped close by rabbits, which shone in the faint twilight with a vivid green that was almost fiery. There was no sound but the murmur of wind and water and the low of homing cattle. There was still some light in the sky, enough to show a multiplicity of cart-tracks, perhaps centuries old, all leading in the same direction. These I followed in open order with the afterglow on my cheek. Faint stars appeared in the zenith, and above the long serrations of Brown Willy mountain a planet hung, bright and sharp as a diamond. The air was keen and cold. I rode in silence, alone with my thoughts. This tranquil movement through an empty world rocked me into a kind of trance, like that induced by sitting too long beside running water or moving tides. I might have been at any place on earth, and at any time in history, since horses were tamed and ridden. I was less myself, more an impersonal traveller under the open sky, looking for a place to pitch my tent and prepare my food.

Devon

It sounds incredible, but trial will show that in this kind of travel you will spend nearly as much time and effort on camp work and packing as on the march itself. No wonder that travellers in outlandish places take hosts of native porters to carry their baggage, and servants to pitch their tents and prepare their food, so that they can devote all their attention to the actual planning and marching, and to the scientific observation, sport, or sheer enjoyment for which they have come. In our kind of travel you have roads and maps and farms and a good climate; but you have also to do all your own animal management, packing, camping, portage, cooking, photography, writing, and surveying, as well as the mere physical activity of getting from one point to another. It is all great fun, but it takes time and effort, and the first few days will always be a trying period of experiment, delay, fatigue, and minor annoyance, in which a lively sense of humour is more valuable than the most foolproof equipment.

Somerset

To a tired and hungry horse traveller, who at the end of a long march had to unpack and prepare his tent and bedding, there is nothing more wearisome than the cooking of supper, and I had made a private resolution that whenever possible I would persuade the farmers' wives to give me tea, with as much to eat as could in decency be asked for.

Most of us never get the maximum of enjoyment out of the common amenities of civilized life, because we are never forced to do without them, and cannot even imagine what life would be like in their absence. To be really appreciated, they must be welcomed like long-lost friends, whom we did not expect to see again. No fatted calf, however fat, will ever seem as good as that which is set before a prodigal son.

Gloucestershire

I rode north quietly and steadily. The afternoon wore on, and I rode in a dream, as if hypnotized by the level road and the brooding trees and quiet cloudy sky. There was no sun, but the light in the west was perceptible, and as we travelled north, it always fell on my left cheek. This was the first time I was definitely aware of it, but each succeeding day at the same time I looked for the light on the left, and thought, we are always moving north, and sooner or later shall be in Scotland.

I always pitied Ladybird for her lack of understanding: she never knew where she would be taken, or whether I planned to keep her trekking for the rest of her natural life. Though I suppose that by this time she had come to associate the setting sun with journey's end and food and grazing. She certainly connected these things with side tracks and farm entrances, for, left to herself, she would always turn right or left sooner than go straight ahead. And she still wished to turn south, little knowing that we were many weary miles from her home in Cornwall.

Derbyshire

It takes some imagination to see that a long ride on horseback, which sounds so thrilling in prospect, may in actual fact be immensely wearisome and mono-tonous, especially with a companion who does not think or act as you do. That is, unless you are a born traveller who can shake down anywhere and with anyone, and these unluckily are rare. So as I lay in my tent I pondered deeply on this problem.

But for a solitary woman nervousness is a luxury that cannot be afforded, and solo travelling has many compensations. You have no one to consider but yourself; you can go where and when you like, stop when you want to, eat what and when you fancy, without reference to the curious and unpredictable tastes of a comrade. You are not really alone, for you have your horse, and everyone is kind to a lone traveller. You get more talk, more friendliness, more hospitality: you see far more of the country. This I expected, and my hopes were confirmed by actual experience. It is wonderful to be riding free as air, and no one to consider but my horse and I.

Yorkshire

No one who wishes to enjoy a riding-tour can afford to be in a hurry. Main-road travelling is hell for horse and rider, and must at all costs be avoided. Many people have asked me how in these days I could manage to dodge traffic. The answer is simple. Keep off all A roads, and as far as possible off the better variety of B road. Most ordinary motor traffic, and all heavy transport, is concentrated on the main thoroughfares, so that on a by-road you can ride for miles without meeting anything but an occasional farm cart, a labourer on his bicycle or the local doctor in his car. The motoring public sticks firmly to the major roads, and hardly knows of the existence of other and less-frequented tracks.

Unfortunately I cannot drive a car myself, so that my experience of motoring problems is one-sided. On the road, I am either a driver of shy mountain sheep, or a leader of nervous horses, or a weary pedestrian, smothered with dust or spattered with mud or choked with fumes, and thus may be excused for having a bias.

As I watched the line of the train curving away towards Stafford, I remembered that in four or five hours time the night express to Scotland would pass this spot, and any sensible traveller would be sitting at ease in a comfortable compartment instead of riding the world with a horse.

Scotland

I could not believe that this was the last day of my journey, which had lasted nearly five weeks, and by this time seemed the normal condition of life. The road was very quiet, and ran for most of its length through woods. I met nothing of note save a man driving sheep, who asked if the mare was for sale. Presently I turned left, and rode down a lane which ended at the white railings of a wayside station. Beyond it was the river Liddel, and on the further bank, Scotland.

So I am at home again. Strathascaig is unchanged, and as it seems, unchangeable. There are of course, some minor innovations. An iron gate has been brought from the riverside pasture to block the Cursing Gap. The old dogs are dead, and there is a new cat. The Laird has grown a little fatter, and Herself a little thinner. But the welcome is the same, and so is the rain.

Yes, the people are the same, and the lasting things – hills, rivers, seas, and skies – remain dominant, with some quality of remoteness, at once restful and stimulating, which will resist the assault of all passing fashions.

And Ladybird, the bay mare who travelled the 560-odd miles between Cornwall and Scotland is the heroine of the piece. When I hitched her to the railing I thought to myself, "Well, that's that; and I am not sorry it's over," while Ladybird, little suspecting that this was the end, cropped the green grass beside the motorway as if ready to spend the rest of her days on the road with me.

These are excerpts from "My Kingdom for a Horse" by Margaret Leigh.

Ladybird.

Chapter 16
My Horse, My Husband and I
by
Ria Bosman Naysmith

We hear a lot of stories at The Long Riders' Guild. People are always recounting various ways that they and their horses rode into, and out of, danger. Attacked by vicious piranha while crossing a river in the Amazon jungle?

Heard that one.

Ambushed by brigands while riding in a Central Asian republic?

Yawn.

Rode over a dangerous mountain?

That's nice.

And then there is Ria Bosman Naysmith.

She sent us the following story, via email, while we were traveling in England to meet other Long Riders. I can still remember the sound of disbelief in Basha's voice when she finished the email and said, "You're not going to BELIEVE this"!

What I discovered was a story that had been painfully recalled, after lying dormant for more than thirty years, and then slowly translated and typed into English instead of Ria's native Afrikaans.

I had to read it, twice, before the story really began to sink in. This wasn't an equestrian expedition - this was a mounted impossibility.

And yes, I'll admit it - we WERE impressed by the fortitude, suffering, and the breath-taking courage shown by Ria, Gordon, and their trusty Lesotho ponies.

That original email is reproduced here now for our readers, the first time this amazing story has appeared in English,

So here is the story of how Ria Bosman, a young South African nurse, teamed up with Gordon Naysmith, Scottish pentathlon athlete, to ride from the tip of South Africa to the Olympics Games being held two years away, in Munich, Germany. The year is 1970. It is late fall when Ria begins her story.

Gordon and I met in hospital where I worked as a physiotherapist. He had a painful back, which I treated. The first thing he said was that his back has to come right because he was going to ride across Africa. Silly me, I thought that sounded great, so somehow I was included. We got married a year later and spent our honeymoon buying horses in the mountains of Lesotho.

The trip started on November 2, 1970 from Maseru, Lesotho. Gordon figured it was more than 20,000 kilometers (14,000 miles) to Munich, Germany. If we kept a tight schedule, we thought we could ride that distance in two years.

The Lesotho pony is probably one of the hardiest horses around. They are not shod, have to find food and water for themselves high up in the mountains. So only the really strong and brave survive the fierce snowy conditions in the winter or droughts that occur every few years. They have no shelter and no veterinary care and no supplementary feeding! That is why we chose them as Africa is a hard, dry, inhospitable place and they would have had to survive it all. The only problem was that due to the altitude they live in, they had no immunity against horse sickness, biliary or any of the other nasty things you get in Africa. All of them got so very sick from their first horse sickness vaccine! The other problem was that very few of them had ever seen a motor car or train. What a circus!

When a motorist honked, all one saw were 11 ponies flying off in 11 different directions. A train nearly drove them berserk! The first 2 weeks we spent hours chasing after panic stricken ponies! Nobody, but nobody who saw us then thought we'll even make it to the Rhodesian border. Must admit, I had my doubts too!

We camped on a farm on the border of Lesotho and South Africa for a few weeks to test the gear, etc. There a young man named Neil Peacock watched this lot in total amazement and very quickly realized I was in great trouble as shouting and screaming by Gordon did not help to teach me how to ride. One day he just came, saddled the ponies (the wildest ones) and took control. His words "Now Ria, this is a horse. That is the front. That is the back. You sit in the middle" – this I will never forget. For hours and hours he took me up and down dongas, up and down mountains, through rivers, etc. etc. He knew my life depended on that. Bless his dear gentle heart – he probably did save my life. He taught me so many little things about the ponies, how to see what each individual liked, how to handle each one, etc.

Travelling through South Africa was pleasant for us, not having to worry about our own needs but very hard for the ponies. The Basutho people mostly ride bare back. So our ponies were not used to saddles or packs on their backs. Riding in the middle of summer did not help very much with the rubbing and saddle sores. Every night all their backs were closely inspected, cold packs put on, rubbing muti (medicine) put on and massaged. Because none of the ponies were shod, all their hooves were cleaned and rubbed with an ointment to strengthen them. All the eyes were cleaned and treated, etc.

The farming community was very helpful and hospitable. That gave us time to get to know the horses and understand them. At first, we hardly ever camped and appreciated a hot bath every night realizing it would soon come to an end.

Our biggest problem was that the kind farmers kept feeding the ponies with real "horse food." They believed we were cruel, but the rest of Africa has no "real food" for the ponies and they had to survive on what they could find in the veldt – as they had done all their lives. We also had to teach them not to drink water when ever they wanted to – only once a day. Again it sounded so cruel but that was the only way to survive in this harsh dry continent where water is a luxury!

The terrorist war was on in Rhodesia and the young policemen at Beitbridge (the border post) took us in for a few days and decided that they were going to do their utmost to keep as alive and they were wonderful. They briefed us on what to do in an attack, what areas to avoid, warned us not to linger at water holes, etc. Right through Rhodesia, the police checked on us during the day, brought us food, etc.

We experienced a heat wave a few days later. The water hole was destroyed by the terrorists so we and the horses had to go without water for 2 days (we only carried 1 liter of water each). The next day, temperatures reached 50 degrees Centigrade (125 Fahrenheit). It was indescribable! The young policemen arrived with a few beers and a liter of water and saved our lives. That day we rode for 12 hours. When we reached a very unfriendly farmer's house, up on a hill, at 7 o'clock at night, the temperature was still 47 degrees Centigrade (115 Fahrenheit). I was in great trouble - totally dehydrated and slightly delirious. Gordon persuaded the nasty man to let us stay the night (Gordon can be very, very convincing) and his kind wife sneaked us oranges, food, and lemon juice. The farmer chased us away the next day.

Fortunately only 10 miles down the road we came to a motel. The owner, a bush-wise, hardened man met us at the side of a swimming pool. Without a word or a greeting he very nonchalantly pushed me into the pool, riding boots and all and "ordered" me to stay there till I was told to get out!! Welcome to Rhodesia! He instructed a waiter to give me a glass of iced water, a little sugar and lemon juice every half hour and he had to watch me drink it all. Very quickly I felt my throat, by now almost totally swollen and closed, getting better, I started seeing in colour again (before I had only been able to only see faint outlines of things) and my hardened, rubber-like skin started getting back to normal. Later that afternoon my rescuer allowed me to get rid of my riding clothes, sleep a little and then ordered me to get back into the pool. This went on for 3 days. But I survived, thanks to this strange, kind man. I never want to see pink elephants and giants ants again!!

In the meantime our poor, poor ponies were suffering just as much. One after another got biliary – all of them! The ones who started eating again then got these terrible runny tummies due to the change in diet. They were used to a hard thin leaved, dry grass and now they ate the luscious wide leaved, juicy grass. What a terrible thing. Fortunately, being the hardy animals they were, they bounced back so quickly. I suppose, not being used to medication at all, even a little bit of the right thing worked immediately. Fortunately half of our packs consisted of muti (medicine) for the horses. The state vet in Lesotho and a few country vets in South Africa saw to it that we had medicine for every possible situation and very clear instructions on what to do in every likely and unlikely situation. These guys were quite incredible, working out in the bush and having to make do under any circumstance.

We took the ponies' pulse rate and temperature every morning and evening. By the time we got to Rhodesia, we knew that 'normal' was different for every pony – up to plus/minus 4 degrees Centigrade. By keeping a clear chart of every pony, one could very quickly see when something went wrong. Biliary had a very specific pattern. One reading would be 2 degrees Centigrade up, the next 3 degrees up then right down to below normal, then the next day, sky high. We were told by the wise vets not to wait for confirmation of blood slides but start injecting with Vitamin B12, Vitamin complex and Berranol immediately. So before the ponies even knew they were ill, we started treatment. That still meant a very sick little pony and days by the side of the road. Only on the second or third day did the eyes and gums turned pale, but by then it would have been too late. When we got to the towns (often about 100 miles apart), we let them take blood samples to make sure that the diagnoses were right.

Biliary is caused by a tick. Later, when we reached Tanzania, there were millions and millions of ticks. One has to see it to believe it. At the waterholes, the grass vibrates because there are thousands of these little monsters waiting for a host to pass by. We had an arsenic dip to wash the horses down with and did this as often as possible. Every morning and evening we scraped hundreds of these ticks off from between the ponies' legs, in their ears, and around their hooves. Dreadful little monsters, those ticks!! At night when we got to bed, we had to examine each other by torch light and pulled off ticks sometimes as many as 50. Both of us got tick bite fever quite a few times – do not believe the story the humans can only get it once – not true at all!!!

The police guys arranged for us to stay at the mounted police stables in Salisbury, Rhodesia (now called Harare, Zimbabwe). They were extremely kind and helpful. They fixed our saddles, backpacks, looked after the horses, their vet did a really thorough examination on every pony and treated them like royalty. But trouble was brewing.   The S.P.C.A. *[Society for the Prevention of Cruelty to Animals]* decided it was cruelty to animals to try and ride our ponies across Africa. They tried by court order to stop us.   This was an embarrassment to the police and their vet, because the private vet hired by the S.P.C.A. to examine the ponies gave a glowing report on the condition of the ponies and took our side. Fortunately the S.P.C.A's attempt failed and we were allowed to continue.   But it was headlines in all the newspapers and on television - even back home in South Africa.

Next big problem – Tsetse fly! We were now entering the real problem areas. During the colonial days these were controlled, but since the war in Rhodesia and Mozambique (now Maputo) it was impossible to control.   Tsetse fly causes Nagana in animals and that is a killer. Fortunately, a vet in Salisbury developed an injection that was in the testing stage.   But this had only been used on cattle, sheep and donkeys, never on horses. The stuff was extremely toxic to humans and absolute care had to be taken in administering this.   Bill, the vet, was very skeptical but we had to take the chance on one of the ponies – three days later the pony was still alive and doing well.   So all the rest were injected too.

Then a few days away from Salisbury new problems started – enormous swellings around the injected area on the neck developed.   Fortunately we were near a phone and Bill came all the way from Salisbury to help. He drained the abscesses, took blood samples, treated the ponies, etc. He reckoned that the injection did the trick, the horses were immune to Nagana and he allowed us to go on very slowly for a few days – he wanted the horses to exercise. (I feared the next lot of injections we were supposed to give a few months later!)

Our next destination was Mozambique. The war there between the rebels and the government was fierce. Frelimo, the terrorist group, controlled the area we were to ride through.   To make matters worse, at the border post the border guards confiscated Gordon's gun with the promise of returning it at the entrance to the next country. But Malawi was a long way to go. Now we were really very vulnerable, especially because the rebels had a notorious way of controlling the "block" we had to ride through. Their method was to kill everything in sight, all birds, reptiles, game, and people. Their motto was "No food - no people"!

Most if not all of Mozambique consists of dense bush, low shrub and very high elephant grass. To get off the road you have to hack your way through the bush.   It was very eerie riding through there!   This long, quiet dirt road, surrounded by thick bush and no natural noise – very scary!! Probably twice a day a big truck would pass us, carrying building material to the Cabora-Bassa dam site. These chappies often stopped to chat and often gave us a cool drink and some fruit. They were probably so happy to see a fellow South African. These trucks got blown up by the rebels on a regular basis and many of the drivers lost their lives. We tried to move through there as quickly as possible and eventually we got to Tete. The story goes that in the olden days the Portuguese government never sent real bad convicts to jail in this colony of Mozambique. They sent them instead to Tete, as being in Tete was much worse than being in jail! I can believe that, as it is said that the humidity there is higher than anywhere in Africa.

When we arrived the Zambezi river was in flood. We saw herds of elephants come floating down the river. What a sight to behold! There was only a ferry across the river and of course we had to wait for the river to get back to normal. The heat and humidity was unbelievable. Everything closes between 12 and 3 o'clock, even the police station. The people at the ferry were very understanding and when the big day arrived they loaded 2 big trucks on either side of the horses and smaller vehicles at both ends and the ponies in the middle. What a nerve racking experience as nobody knew what the ponies were going to do with this rolling, strange moving thing they were on.

Fortunately everything went well to the other side, but then they refused to go down the gangplanks. One of the ponies cut his leg very badly and we had to go and fetch a vet back in Tete, hours later the pony was fixed. Unfortunately we then were forced to stay in a little town that was notorious for terrorist attacks. We had no choice as the little pony's leg was so very painful. What was worse, we had to stay in the police station grounds where most of the attacks took place. That night the terrorists blew up a truck between the ferry and the town and one on the other side of the town. Even the ponies could sense the tension in the air. But again we were so very blessed and got to the Malawian boarder without any mishap.

Malawi, or as it is known, the land of the smiling faces, was very pleasant: One cannot believe that some imaginary line between two countries can make such a big difference to people. One almost felt uncomfortable because somebody was always smiling or laughing at you, lovely people, so very helpful and so eager to learn about the ponies.

What a surprise to find my parents waiting for us at Blantyre. They drove all that way to come and see us. At that stage one could not fly from South Africa to anywhere in Africa, and they faced all the dangers through Rhodesia and Mozambique. The ponies needed their second horse sickness vaccines also and that meant a three week rest for them. The South African vaccine lasts for a year and the Russians insisted on a 6 monthly injection and two of the ponies got very sick and one died, how very, very sad.   The other little one pulled through, thankfully.

My parents took us to the lake for a holiday, and it was bliss sleeping in a clean bed every night and the wonderful luxury of bathing each evening. It is amazing how much one can do with liter of water, cooking one's food, cleaning all the necessary bodily parts and washing undergarments and brushing teeth!! So by that stage clean running water from a tap was an enormous luxury. Even today my stomach turns when I think of the water we had to drink at times, water scooped from waterholes with green slime a few inches thick, and animal dung in it. Thank heaven for the water sterilizing tablets the Rhodesians gave us. I think we would have died without them.

Fruit in Malawi is plentiful and very cheap, so we ate very well. The local people also were so very eager to share their meals with us and so often arrived with a few eggs, tomatoes, cassava, a local vegetable, or any thing else. Some of the villagers also allowed us to let the ponies graze their left over maize fields. The locals were absolutely marvellous. But because the little children ran with us for miles on end - it was difficult to find a spot where one could be private when nature called!

One day we camped just outside a little village, and I woke up feeling a little dizzy. When we finished packing up I was in trouble. The 2 miles into the next village took ages. We rode to the mission hospital where I collapsed and fell off the pony. A man who had just got out of his jeep, caught me. He happened to be a young French doctor who was doing research on a new strain of malaria, called galloping malaria. He was collecting samples miles out in the bush and had to return to fetch something he forgot. I was one of the first Europeans to get "galloping malaria." Apparently this type of malaria kills people in two days. So it was very fortunate for me that this young man knew what to do and helped me. I was very, very sick for the next few days. In Malawi they had government rest houses in a few small towns and we were fortunate enough to have stayed in one of those. I think if we had had to stay in our small tent in the bush somewhere things would have been different for me.

After we crossed into Tanzania we started seeing a lot of wild life. The animals did not seem to recognise the human shape on the ponies, so we could ride very close to a lot of them. But it was also lion country. We often heard them, sometimes uncomfortably close! The elephants did not like the look of this new form of wild life and we had to move very carefully and very quickly out of their sight.

The main road goes through a game park and we had to follow that road. One night we went to a lodge in the park to see if we could camp on their premises and this German fellow was so very rude and chased us away. An African man who realized we were in trouble came to our rescue. He told us to ride to a shed a few miles away. There we would be more safe than just out in the bush. When we got there we discovered that the river a few hundred yards away from the shed was the drinking place for all the large game. These animals were already arriving at the waterhole because the sun was setting. But this German fellow contacted the police. Whilst we were unpacking about 12 of them came with big guns and bayonets. They started shouting and screaming, threw everything we had out on the floor of the shed, opened the cameras, and ordered us in to their jeeps. We drove at an unbelievable speed in the dark cross country to their police station. They forced Gordon to stand up in this jeep. He fell and broke a few ribs, but they could not care less. They locked us up till the next day when the big boss would arrive. We were so very worried about the ponies alone out there with the lions around!

The big boss arrived and interrogated us for hours. We were suppose to be Israeli spies! Can you believe that? Luckily, before we started our trip Chief Jonathan, the prime minister of Lesotho, gave us a letter of introduction. It was this slip of paper that saved our lives. Gordon made such a big scene and told them that there were going to be a big war between Tanzania and Lesotho if anything happened to "Chief Jonathan's horses." Fortunately they believed him. They took us back to the horses and ordered us out of the park in two hours: it took nearly two days. The kind African man who helped us in the first place had taken it upon himself to look after the ponies whilst we were in jail. We left as soon as possible but Gordon was in great pain and we moved slowly.

Then it got worse, and was a little scary, because we realized that lions were following us. Before leaving, the people in the know had assured us that lions will not attack a "smell" they are not used to. Our only hope was to forget Gordon's pain, keep moving, not stay in one place for two nights in a row, and hope the "experts" were right!!!

There was a great drought in Tanzania in 1971 and everything went hungry, including the ponies. We fed them on what ever grain we could buy from the locals. By then they had grown used to eating anything that even looked like food. Poor darlings !!

Then we arrived at a little village late one afternoon. The headman said we could stay. The only problem was that a pack of hyenas raided this village every night. The headman said we were welcome to share a little building that had a corrugated iron roof. This was important because the hyenas climbed on top of the huts and broke through grass roofs to get to anything eatable inside. So Gordon and I and all of our ponies were bundled into one the few huts with a metal roof. We were huddled in there with all their chickens and small animals and a big fire was started to keep the beasts away. It was so very scary when the hyenas arrived. They make that horrible noise when they scream and laugh. When the little ponies heard the hyenas, they became frantic with fear and so were we. The beasts charged the door, climbed on top of the roof, scratched the corrugated iron with their long nails, doing everything to try to get to the ponies and eat them. It was very terrible. Fortunately by morning the hyenas left and we could move on as far as possible from that fearful place.

At Iringa, Tanzania I suspected that I might be pregnant. I saw a doctor from India. But he was not sure, so we had to move on. A few days later I started bleeding. Strange how every time one of us was in trouble help just seemed to arrive out of nowhere. This time in the form of a Italian man who was working on a new road near by. He directed us to their road camp. When we arrived I was bleeding a lot. The man who found us went ahead to tell the people there of our coming and the men, not the few woman, were waiting with blankets for us. They so very gently covered my blood drenched body and escorted me to the loo. They removed my clothes, stacked pillows all around the loo, and there I sat like a queen on a throne! Strange how love does not speak in a language, as they could not speak any English and I, not a word of Italian. The message was clear, they were going to help me no matter what, and they did with more care than I could have received at a hospital. They washed my clothes, put me in bed and really cared for me so well. I will never ever forget these rough, hardened men with their calloused hands, sun-baked faces, and kind, gentle hearts. They saved my life, without any doubt. The ponies got a nice rest, good food and their condition improved a lot at that camp. Gordon took the time to fix everything that was broken, so it was a good rest for all.

We reached Mount Kilimanjaro on the far side of Tanzania and stayed with the honorary German consul and his family. What an experience to wake up every morning and see that incredible mountain, every day a different sight. I think every person on earth should see that once in their lifetime. It is the most beautiful experience one can imagine. These kind people had horses and our ponies stayed with them and had a feast after the drought-stricken areas we had come through.

At that stage we did not have permission to enter, or ride through Kenya yet. But trust Gordon. If one cannot go round something you go through it, no matter what it costs or what tactics you use. In the nearby city of Arusha, the government officials of Kenya said "no" in no uncertain terms to the idea of letting us ride across their country. But after "negotiating" very long and hard (which of course also included Gordon's threat of the big war that would result between them and the tiny kingdom of Lesotho if they tried to stop us!) they agreed we may enter. But, and a big BUT, only if we can show proof from a vet that the ponies had no contact with any other horse or any other animal that carries foot-and-mouth disease during the entire trip from Lesotho! They thought this was obviously an impossible task and this requirement would keep us and the ponies out of Kenya forever.

Again, nothing stops Gordon. The next day when the director of veterinary services for Tanzania was away on business, which Gordon knew, he stormed into the deputy's office shouted and screamed and made such a big scene. The poor chap was so confused, he signed all the papers we needed and before anybody could change their minds we were on our way out of Tanzania. We made a flying visit to say goodbye to the kind German consul at his wonderful coffee plantation. Then we were riding on our way to the border.

Our stay at Arusha had been the most pleasant of the whole trip. We left there with heavy hearts and travelled through the bush to avoid any possibility of being caught and sent back by the authorities of either Tanzania or Kenya. We headed for a tiny border post in the middle of nowhere and the man let us through without any trouble! On the way I got sunstroke very badly and again was really very sick. But we had to go on as food for the ponies was again very scarce and Gordon wanted to get to Nairobi as soon as possible as we were now very badly behind schedule. Luckily, the German consul in Arusha had contacted the Lesotho ambassador in Nairobi, and told him about our predicament with the authorities of Kenya.

Imagine our surprise when we rode up to the edge of Nairobi, where we were stopped by somebody from the Lesotho office and told to go to the show grounds. This kind reception was strange to us. On our arrival a whole bunch of people welcomed us, including the wonderful Lesotho ambassador and his lovely wife, and of course all the newspapers. This was a big set-up to keep us in the country, I suspect. This lovely man and his wife took us into their home and made arrangements for the ponies.

All dressed up in clothes borrowed from the ambassador and his lady, we attended a Lesotho independence celebration party. There I fainted and was stone cold out for an hour or so. Fortunately a lovely Indian lady doctor attended the party and took care of me. I had to go and see her a few times and she did all sorts of tests on me. She said the malaria was not cured yet, the infection from the miscarriage was still with me, and the after affects of the sunstroke etc. etc. all made it necessary for me to go home to South Africa. Gordon felt I could go on if we could get a wagon and let the ponies pull it!!

Anyway, a team of people working on a set of a play they were producing, decided to build the wagon, which they did. This time Gordon bit off more than he could chew as the poor, poor ponies just could not learn to pull that damned wagon. So he decided to go on alone. In a way I was sad as I really wanted to go with all the way to the Olympics in Germany with him.

So, we gave my ponies to a lovely man, and Gordon took three with him and left for Addis Ababa, Ethiopia, and I came home to my wonderful parents in South Africa.

The rest of the story is Gordon's story and he will probably tell you how he rode through the Arabian deserts and all the other things that happened to him before he finally reached Europe.

We are happy to announce that Gordon Naysmith is now working on a book about this extraordinary equestrian journey. Entitled, "A Will to Win", it will be published by The Long Riders' Guild Press prior to Gordon's departure from London on a round-the-world canoe trip.
Ria meanwhile lives quietly, without horses, in South Africa.

Ria Bosman Naysmith and Louis, Norton, Gordon Naysmith and Essex.

Chapter 17
Riding from the Flames
by
Lady Florence Dixie

When asked in 1879 why she wanted to journey to such an outlandish place as Patagonia, the author replied without hesitation that she was taking to the saddle in order to flee from the strict confines of polite Victorian society.

"Palled for the moment with civilization and its surroundings, I wanted to escape somewhere, where I might be as far removed from them as possible. Many of my readers have doubtless felt the dissatisfaction with oneself, and everybody else, that comes over one at times in the midst of the pleasures of life; when one wearies of the shallow artificiality of modern existence; when what was once excitement has become so no longer, and a longing grows up within one to taste a more vigorous emotion than that afforded by the monotonous round of society's so called pleasures."

As her story aptly illustrates, Lady Florence successfully traded the perils of a London parlor for the wind-borne freedom of a wild Patagonian bronco.

As we rode along, our attention was attracted by a faint smell of burning, and presently thick clouds of smoke came rolling toward us. We pressed wonderingly on, anxious to discover the whereabouts of the fire, which we trusted lay somewhere far from our camp. Reaching a slight eminence, we were able to command a view of the country ahead. A cry of dismay escaped our lips as we looked around, and drawing rein, we stared blankly at one another. A fearful sight lay before us. To our left, right in front, and gradually wreathing the hills to our right, a huge prairie fire came rushing rapidly along. Dense masses of smoke curled aloft, and entirely obscured the sky; the flames, which shot fiercely up, cast a strange yellow glare over everything. Even whilst we watched, a strong gust of wind swept the fire with incredible swiftness towards us, and in a second we were enveloped in such a dense cloud of smoke that we were unable to see one another.

The situation had now become critical, and not a moment was to be lost. Half-choked, and bewildered by the suddenness with which the danger had come upon us, we scarcely knew what course to take. Already our horses were snorting with fear, as the crackling of the burning grass and bushes came nearer and nearer. To run away from the coming fire was useless; the alternative was to face it at a gallop and get through it if possible. To throw our capes over our heads, and draw them as tightly round us as we could, was the work of a second, and then digging our spurs into our horses, we dashed forward, every rider for themselves.

The moments that followed seemed an eternity. As I urged my unwilling horse forward, the sense of suffocating grew terrible, I could scarcely breathe, and the panting animal seemed to stagger beneath me. The horrible crackling came nearer and nearer; I became conscious of the most intolerable heat, and my head began to swim round. My horse gave two or three furious plunges, and then burst madly forward. Almost choked, come what might, I could bear the cape over my head no longer, and tore it off me.

The sudden sense of relief that came over me as I did so, I shall never forget. I looked up, the air was comparatively clear, and the fire behind me. By some miracle I had passed through it unhurt. I looked for my companions, and, to my inexpressible joy, saw them emerge one by one from the black mass of smoke, which was now rapidly receding into the distance.

Congratulations and exclamations over, we retraced our steps to try and discover how we had managed to escape so luckily. The reason was soon apparent. By a piece of fortune we had happened to ride over a narrow pebbly tract of ground, where the grass was extremely sparse, and where there were but few bushes; had chance led us over any other track where the grass was thick and tall, we could scarcely ever have got through the danger. Our poor horses had suffered a good deal as it was, their feet and legs being scorched and singed severely.

Our thoughts flew to our camp, and to our servants Storer and I'Aria, whom we had left behind there. That they had escaped we had little doubt, but for our tents and luggage we felt there was no hope. The landscape seemed completely changed by the fire, all around, as far as we could see, stretched smoking plains, and the outlines of the hills had become quite unfamiliar to us. With rather heavy hearts we pushed forward, eagerly scanning the country for some indication which might guide us to the quarter where our camp had stood. If, as we had every reason to believe, our things were burnt, our Patagonian trip was at an end.

Fortunately things did not turn out so badly. Presently my husband, who was riding in advance of the others, gave a shout, and made signals for us to come on. I need hardly say that we did not lose a moment in joining him, and a welcome sight, as we got up to him, met our eyes.

Some two or three hundred yards below the hill on which we were, we perceived our little white tents standing safe and unharmed on a narrow green tract of land, which looked like a smiling island in the midst of the vast black plain. Storer and I'Aria, too, we could see moving about, and, overjoyed, we galloped down towards them, they running out to meet us, having suffered no little anxiety, on their parts, as to what might have happened to us. We passed question after question to I'Aria and Storer as to how they had managed to save the camp. Storer was unable to give any intelligible account, so entirely upset was he by fright, but I'Aria's natural philosophical calm had not deserted him, even on this occasion, and from him we heard all the particulars. The fire, he informed us, had been caused by the Indian we had met in the morning, who was on the look-out for stray horses. This man had amused himself by setting fire to the long dry grass in various places, and, fanned by a strong wind, the flames spread, and soon assumed enormous proportions.

Quick to perceive the possible danger our camp was in, the Indian at once galloped up, and with the assistance of I'Aria and Storer, set about making a "contra-fuego" or counter-fire; that is to say, they gradually set fire to the grass all around the camp, letting it burn a considerable tract, but always keeping it well in subjection, beating it out with bushes and trampling it under foot, so that it could not get beyond their control. This precautionary measure was fortunately completed by the time the big fire came on, and, although, for a minute or two, they were half suffocated by the smoke, the fire passed harmlessly by the camp itself.

Our extra horses were all safe, as they had been grazing on the far side of a stream in an adjacent valley. Nevertheless the camp was in great disorder; the tents were blackened by the smoke, the provision bags and other chattels lay scattered in confusion. Our furs and rugs had been used to cover the cartridges with, for whilst the fire raged around it, the camp was deluged by showers of sparks, and an explosion might have easily occurred had this precaution not been taken. For some time we were busy putting things straight, and in the meanwhile Francois arrived from his hunting excursion.

Dinner over, my companions were not long before they went to sleep, but feeling little inclination to follow their example, I strolled out, and wandered round the camp, watching with interest the strange changes that came over the landscape as day waned and night came slowly on. The black hills behind the camp loomed like shadowy phantoms against the sky; far and wide slept the silent pampa, its undulating surface illuminated by the rays of a lovely moon. The faint glow which tinged its horizon, and the strange noises which a puff of wind occasionally brought to my ears, showed that the mighty fire was still burning in the distance with unabated fury, perhaps not to stop in its devastating course till it reached the sea-coast, many miles away.

For a long time I stood immersed in the contemplation of this weird desolate scene, giving myself up to the mysterious feelings and the many vague and fanciful thoughts it suggested, till, overcome with the excitement and exertions of the day, I had at last to give way to drowsiness and seek my repose.

This is an excerpt from "Riding Across Patagonia" by Lady Florence Dixie.

The author and her husband.

Chapter 18
Khyber Knights
by
CuChullaine O'Reilly

Experience has taught me that you are seldom prepared for what you discover while exploring the world from the back of a horse.

Despite your best laid plans and previous equestrian experience, when you venture out onto the road the rules you previously lived by are the first thing you learn to jettison. Nothing is how it should be. The weather turns vile. You struggle to speak the language adequately. You can't find food and shelter for yourself and your mount. Someone is always trying to rob, trick, cajole, convert, kidnap, befuddle or bewitch you. Your horse gets sick. Then you get sick and start to think about your bones moldering in some ignoble backwater grave.

Why, you ask yourself, did it come to this? What brought you to find yourself in another desperate situation?

I know the answer because I too have heard the tune that lures us from sweet home and warm hearth. For like the other riders in this book I have listened to the seductive siren song of the saddle! Yes, I am no different. If this book has fools in it I humbly take my place among them. I have made every mistake listed on these pages, including the folly of setting out in the first place. I am a master at ignoring the strident urgings of reason and common sense .

Case in point was my trip in 1983. I had already ridden on four continents and prided myself on knowing horsemen from Texas to Tibet. I was a spurred potpourri of international equestrian experiences, full of a false confidence based upon the rules of the world as I understood it. I believed I was ready to make my first solo horse trip, a journey through the treacherous tribal territory of northern Pakistan. Setting out from my adopted home in Peshawar, Pakistan I was traveling under my Moslem name, Asadullah Khan. Beneath the old British military saddle was a fine palomino mare, Shavon. Stashed under my black turban were still a great many naive, youthful dreams; a situation Pakistan, that harsh mistress of my equestrian life, immediately set about rectifying.

It seemed like a good idea at the time. Buy a horse in Peshawar, Pakistan, then head north on my own to the remote and distant province of Chitral. There I planned to team up with members of the mujahadeen, Afghan resistance fighters, who were locked in a deadly struggle with the armed might of the Soviet Union.

The jihad, or war of liberation, was going very badly for the Afghans in 1983. Russian Hind-24 helicopter gun-ships controlled the skies over a country I had once ridden through and still remembered fondly. The mujahadeen were out-gunned, out-manned and demoralized. Every week new posters were plastered around Peshawar showing photos of the latest shaheed, or martyred mujahadeen, who had marched home to fight, only to die a few days later.

Despite their legendary bravery the average mujahadeen was poorly armed and even more poorly led. The leaders of the seven resistance groups were at each other's throats. The only thing they could agree on was that after killing the atheist Russians, they would turn their knives on each other. To make matters worse, Peshawar had become part of the war zone. Sitting at the mouth of the famous Khyber Pass, the ancient walled city had more spies than occupied Berlin. In addition, its twisting streets were crowded with a human cocktail of bombers, mercenaries, holy warriors, expatriate aid workers and hundreds of thousands of Afghan refugees. As a journalist it was my job to swim around in this climate of intrigue and deceit.

My old friend Pirgumber Kul, a Turkoman mujahadeen commander, was the one who gave me the idea to head north and join up with horsemen from his tribe. According to Pirgumber's sources in the resistance, a large group of muja-hadeen from his tanzim (resistance organization) were to rendezvous in Chitral, where they would procure arms and ammunition. Famed for their equestrian skills, the Turkomans would welcome another horseman, Pirgumber told me.

I was hungry for more adventure, especially one that included such notorious mounted warriors. Besides, I reasoned, I was ready. The journey north from Peshawar to Chitral would be my third equestrian trip in that part of Asia. Of course no one had ridden it on horseback since 1937, when the last mounted British army patrol rode down to Peshawar, and returned via armored car. But I wasn't going to let that stop me; nor the idea that this time I would be riding alone until I located Pirgumber's comrades, several hundred miles away. Using contacts among the local Pathan tribesmen, I bought a fine palomino mare and an old British cavalry saddle. The ancient Webley revolver I had purchased surrep-titiously in the bazaar, along with my counterfeit mujahadeen identity card, I placed in the bottom of my Afghan saddlebags. With a hoof-pick for the horse and a copy of "War and Peace" for me, I set off into the unknown.

It was a hell of a beginning. The weather was as hot as a blowtorch. The Pathan tribes I passed through were suspicious. The mare soon developed a limp in her off fore. And I still had hundreds of miles to go.

But it was my Irish roots that nearly got me killed. Before leaving Peshawar, I had an artist friend of mine paint a large red hand on the right shoulder of Shavon, my mare. This totem of Irish defiance had represented the O'Reillys for centuries. Considering the journey into war-torn Afghanistan that lay ahead of me, it seemed appropriate to fly it again. Besides, I was too naive to realize it could be interpreted as being anything but Gaelic.

The sun was threatening to boil my brains inside my turban when I rode into a nameless, fly-blown village. Alongside the road was a shack just big enough for one man to squat in. A scrub tree threw a spattering of shade over the hovel. Sitting outside the doorway on a charpoy (native rope bed) were three crusty characters. I didn't pay any attention to these relics; all I could see was the ancient icebox full of cold soft drinks.

I pulled the mare up. A quick glance told me that the nearby village was an Afghan refugee camp. Even at that distance the place stank of despair. I asked the shopkeeper for an orange soda. He obliged by handing one up to me in the saddle. One of the three Afghans sitting on the charpoy started to question me before I had the bottle drained.

"Who are you?"

"Asadullah Khan, an American Moslem."

"Where are you bound for?"

"Chitral."

"Why?"

"I'm going to meet friends there."

"Why?"

"Personal business."

That's when things started to take a sudden wrong turn. In defense of these strangers, it wasn't a bad idea to be suspicious of a white-skinned traveler dressed in loose Afghan clothes and a turban. Both the KGB and KHAD, the Afghan communist secret police, had informers in all the mujahadeen organizations. Spying was rampant and assassination was common. In such an atmosphere of treachery no one trusted their neighbor, much less a foreigner on a horse.

But I never got the chance to explain. Suddenly the inquisitive man closest to me on the charpoy stood up. His face had been partly melted away by a napalm blast. He was ugly and belligerent. It was an unfortunate meeting.

"Get down," he ordered.

I tossed money towards the shopkeeper.

"Thanks, but I must be going."

"Look at this!" he said triumphantly, pointing at the red hand he had discovered painted on Shavon's shoulder. Here was hard evidence of my communist collusion.

"You're a Russian spy! Get down!" he screamed, and grabbing the reins below the bit, tried to gain control of my horse.

I could stand a lot; the heat, this ignorant peasant, even his misplaced suspicions. But no one messes with my horse.

I snapped.

"You dog!" I yelled at him, then slashed him with my quirt. I set spurs to the horse and trampled him into the dust like a rag. The mare charged out of town. It didn't seem like the time or place to discuss the history of Irish resistance symbology.

We rode hard for fifteen minutes. Yet the weather was fierce, and Shavon was soon drenched in sweat. I slowed her to a walk, patted her neck, assuring her that in the future I would be more careful about where I bought soft drinks. The motor traffic of the country road was steady and I wasn't paying much attention, until a large Toyota van sped by me, then came to a sliding stop sideways, blocking the road. Before I realized what was happening, the doors flew open and a crowd of men, including my former inquisitor, came rushing at me.

"Kushad dushman mukbir (Kill the enemy spy)," they were screaming.

Then hands were reaching up, trying to drag me to the ground. I started whipping them with my quirt, at the same time trying to keep Shavon under control and stay in the saddle. But then time seemed to stop. I froze as my vision narrowed in on an old man striding toward me from the van. His face was full of fear and his gun hand was shaking. The pistol he was holding was staring at me with its huge, evil looking black hole. I waited for him to fire, and told myself, "This is where I die."

Before the old man could take aim and fire, I was swept off my horse by the crowd of shouting men. The wizened ancient gunman made his way through the crowd and held the pistol on me, while various members of the mob started to beat me. I tried to cover my face with my arm. Luckily my turban took most of the impact from the blows aimed at my head.

There was no point in trying to talk. These fellows were shouting back and forth and clearly out for my blood. Shavon's reins were ripped out of my hands. Then the old gunman shoved his pistol into my back and motioned for me to move away from my horse. I hesitated for a moment, then someone gave me a terrific shove in the back.

I had no choice. I started walking back toward the refugee camp, and a dangerously uncertain future.

During this episode the motor traffic was forced to slow to a crawl in order to pass both the mob and their van, which was still sitting sideways across the rural highway. As I walked, I was surrounded by my antagonists, but I could clearly see the motorists as they went slowly by, staring awkwardly at me, the guns, and my angry captors.

When I noticed a shiny black car pull alongside, I discerned that the passenger in the back was a well-to-do Pakistani being transported by his chauffeur. Instantly, I decided to take a chance.

"Help! Stop your car! Stop your car! I'm being kidnapped!" I shouted in English at the passenger, while struggling to break free of my captors.

Though my shouts brought a rain of blows to my back and head, my kidnappers were out of luck. I saw the Pakistani motion to his driver to pull over. He quickly got out and came walking toward us.

"What's going on here?" he asked in the British-accented English of the educated upper classes. I reached under my shirt and produced my American passport from a hidden leather bag, then summed up the situation to this good Samaritan, a government official on his way from Timagura, the provincial capital, back to Peshawar.

"The bloody cheek of these refugees," he said when he heard my explanation. He then began to berate my abductors in a torrent of abusive Pushtu, casting aspersions on the chastity of their mothers and commenting on the ignorance of these sons of the Khyber Pass.

"I've told them that as refugees they are guests in my country, as are you, and as Moslems it is a disgrace to treat one of our American brothers with such disrespect. I've ordered them to release you immediately or I will be forced to bring in the police," he told me.

Meanwhile, the aforementioned guns had begun to disappear, and the van suddenly came alongside. My former captors were making noises as if they were sorry. I didn't take more than a second to grab Shavon's reins back from the ignorant villager who had been eyeing her greedily. I vaulted into the saddle, then turned to thank my rescuer.

"Don't worry. They'll leave you alone for the time being. But I wouldn't trust them when I'm gone. Go at once and don't slow down until you reach Dargai," he told me. I didn't need to be encouraged. I set spurs to the mare and fled toward the safety of the nearby mountains. As I rode away, it dawned on me that I had never asked my rescuer his name.

It was a tense night. The village of Dargai didn't even have a chaikhana (teahouse) that could shelter us. With the possibility of my former abductors showing up at any minute to exact their revenge, Shavon and I pushed on into the dark, not knowing what lay ahead. Thinking that a village or some manner or rest was still within reach, we continued mile after weary mile through the desolate, darkened countryside.

When the road started climbing into the mountains, I simply followed it, not realizing I was leading the tired mare and myself up the mighty Malakand Pass. Just before dawn we found a tree with enough level ground under it for the two of us to throw down our dead-tired bones and rest. We crossed the top of the Malakand Pass the next morning, and pressed ever-northward toward the elusive Turkoman mujahadeen contacts I was to meet in Chitral. Though my tormentors of the previous day never did reappear, the following days were filled with new challenges.

Soon the Lowari Pass blocked our way. When we saw this 10,500 foot wall of solid rock rearing up into the blue Pakistani sky, we knew the hot days of the plains were behind us. Ahead lay an ocean of mountains, deep with distance, a silent sea of unbroken stony waves.

After I bought supplies in the village of Dir, Shavon and I pushed straight uphill for seven and a half hours before we finally managed to reach the icy, wind-swept crest of the Lowari. The wind was howling up there, determined to sweep us off this secret place he protected. Far ahead I caught a glimpse of Tirich Mir, the highest peak in the bastion of the Hindu Kush mountains. To the west lay Afghanistan, to the east lay Yaghistan the land of murder, behind me lay heartache, ahead lay Chitral.

Lying waiting below was a mountainside utterly different from that which we had just climbed. Where as that had been gradual, this was a hair-raising apology of a track. It was barely wide enough to accommodate one vehicle and ran back and forth in zigzags so deep I could only guess at their ending. Deodars and pines clothed the steep slopes. The road lay daring, so on we went.

Down and down we dropped. Here on this hidden slope the mountain was pitiless and untamed. Treacherous landslides hovered above us. Chasms were revealed. We came to understand that nothing we had seen matched the hard impersonal cruelty of these dangerous mountains. I sat my saddle, prayed to Allah and gave the mare her head, listening to the sickening sounds of her hooves sliding on loose rocks. A slip here, a body out of true and death lay waiting with its open, bottomless maw. If they thought to think us missing, I doubt they could have found us.

That night, safe on level ground, I berthed in a tent with a group of Pakistani soldiers sent to clear rock slides off the road. The next morning they urged me to turn back, telling me that snow leopards would surely eat my mare if we continued. I thanked them for the advice, and the tea-and-bread breakfast, and rode on.

Days and nights, and village after village, passed by. I grew close to my goal of reaching Chitral and meeting the Afghan freedom fighters who would take me into their war-torn country. But the weary miles had taken their toil on both the mare and me. She looked thin and tired; I felt beat. But I had an option.

Before reaching Chitral, I could turn off for rest in the side-valleys of Kafiristan, the home of a group of natives who were the last living relics of a former pagan empire. Supposedly descended from soldiers of the army of Alexander the Great, the Kalashi had a mixed reputation among Pakistan's devout Moslems.

But I was not on any mercy mission. I aimed to take my horse and myself into the wilds of Afghanistan. I knew that before that struggle began we both needed rest. Plus the Kalash had grass in their valleys. Lots of it! I came to the canyon that led west, towards Kafiristan. To hell with theology. I headed Shavon away from my Moslem brothers in Chitral and on towards a well-earned respite, pagan or not.

They say in Pakistan that Allah knows better about all things. Perhaps that is why events happened the way they did there. Shavon and I followed a twisting track that lead into a deep canyon. When it eventually opened, it revealed a beautiful valley, peopled by kind Kalashi farmers, smiling mothers and laughing children. I found a tiny inn in a Kalashi village. A magnificent river flowed close by my room. Shavon was up to her belly in the pasture full of succulent grass I had bought her. Everywhere I looked I saw an Arcadian paradise.

Despite this welcoming oasis, I felt lethargic. Within a couple of days I started getting chills and came down with a fever. I shrugged it off, having already been sick from just about every germ known to man. Just amebic dysentery again, I told myself.

Then I started to throw up after eating my dinner one night. The next morning I was woozy, and could barely walk to the pasture, or take Shavon to the river for a drink. At that point I started to get a little concerned. I had reason to. It only got worse.

The next morning I was so weak I could barely sit up. Then I threw up my breakfast tea. It seemed like my stomach was going into convulsions. I staggered back to my bed and passed out.

I awoke early the following day, lying on the bed, soaked in sweat. I could hear Shavon neighing frantically.

"She must be thirsty," I thought, and then tried to sit up. I couldn't. In fact, I was so weak I couldn't move a muscle. I laid there going in and out of a state of delirious consciousness. Slowly my vision narrowed on my right hand.

"Close your fingers. Just close your fingers," I told myself.

It was impossible. I couldn't summon up the energy to even do this simple task. I heard the hotel owner passing outside my door, but I was too weak to call out for help. Once again, I passed out and drifted down into a black hole of sickness.

Well after dark the inn-keeper gently shook me awake. He told me he had watered Shavon, then put her back in the pasture. In a whisper I explained how sick I was. He agreed to fetch the village medic in the morning.

Help of sorts came with the rising sun. The local school teacher who arrived was also the resident medic. His medical degree was granted based upon the fact that he could read the words on the prescription bottle. He was well-meaning, but ill-equipped to deal with an illness he couldn't diagnose. His determination was that I suffered from "general weakness." The prescription, an intravenous drip of glucose water.

As the sugar water slowly entered my veins I knew I was dying, knew for certain something was killing me by slow degrees. If I stayed in this backwards village I'd end up being buried by my pagan attendants. My greatest worry had always been dying in some forgotten corner of the world and getting my bones dumped into a nameless hole.

The nearest real help was in Chitral, a hard day's ride, and at least thirty miles away through a sandy, mountainous no-man's land. I didn't have a choice. I knew what I had to do. It was go there or die here.

When the drip finished I felt surprisingly better. I had the inn-keeper bring Shavon around and saddle her. He threw my saddlebags on her back, filled my canteen and gave me two aspirins as a going-away present. Then he and the "doctor" helped me mount.

It must have been the glucose. I was light-headed, but coherent for the first time in days. I waved goodbye and headed down the valley, toward help. My condition didn't take long to catch up with me. Within a couple of hours I was wracked with a blinding headache. I swallowed the aspirins with a slug of warm canteen water.

Wrong !!!

I felt like I had been poisoned. My stomach revolted and threw it back up. I slumped in the saddle, heaving, my fingers locked around the pommel to keep from falling off. Humiliated, I wiped the spittle off my face. After that I just settled in and kept going. I was ill but felt like I was still in control.

After several hours Shavon and I made it down the canyon, hit the main dirt road and then turned left, heading north toward Chitral and safety. We passed into a isolated, uninhabited, desert country, all gray rock, gray dust and the gray water of the Chitral river. The world was all gray now except the sun. It was white hot and hammering me mercilessly. The river lay far down a steep, slanting cliff face, well below the road. I could hear its roar, could see it so close. I was very thirsty and was sure the water must be cool. I told myself not to be a fool. If I managed to get down there, I wouldn't have the strength to climb back up. Some strong instinct warned me at that instant that I had to stay in the saddle at all costs, that my survival was dependent on remaining with my horse.

Shavon took me on, the two of us traveling through an uninhabited land of heat and heartbreak. The silence was deafening. There was the roar of the river, the soft plodding of the mare's hooves in the thick muffling dust. But those sounds seemed to lie outside the world I was traveling in. Somewhere I heard a soft little song floating high off. Shavon was by now directing her own course. I was holding the reins but they lay limp in my fingers. I had given up all conscious thought of being in charge of the mare. The sun had reduced me to a lump of warm baggage. All I could concentrate on was the soft song I could hear coming from far away. The sun was so bright, and my eyes hurt so badly. I wanted to close them for just a brief second. That little song kept nagging me. I had heard it somewhere before.

"Oh, it is the saddle creaking," I realized and smiled at my foolishness.

That is the last thought I remembered clearly. Then the bad times started. I began to slide in and out of consciousness, delirious one moment, weak but cognizant the next. I could feel myself starting to sway in the saddle. The sunlight pounded inside my head, causing a fire-flecked pain to blind me. I simply had to close my eyes.

The next thing I experienced was the taste of dry, thick dust in my mouth. I could feel my breath coming very slowly. I realized I was lying face down on my stomach. I could feel the hot, sun-baked dirt of the road under my palms. I opened my eyes. I had fainted, slipped from the saddle and fallen to the ground. I groaned, managed to sit up and saw Shavon standing patiently over me. Her reins were trailing in the dust as she partly shielded me from the sun.

To this day I have no idea how long I had been lying in that road. It could have been seconds or hours. It did not matter to the mare. Her rider lay motionless. This was a difficulty she could not resolve alone. So she stood over me, waiting for her horseman to make a decision for us both, waiting for guidance. If she had left me I would have died. It's that simple. It's that true.

I'll never know how I got back on the saddle. When I looked up at Shavon I saw an unbearable look in her eye, an almost human expression of anxious concern. That look helped. I knew I only had enough strength for one supreme effort.

I grasped the stirrup iron and pulled. I rose so slowly I wasn't sure I could make it. She stood there like a patient cowboy pony, her legs spread, her head up, an immovable rock of support. I struggled up, got to my feet, stood there swaying, a filthy, dusty mess of a man. I leaned against her warm, moist hide, grabbed the saddle and then heaved myself up onto the hurricane deck with no pretense at grace.

I felt naked and alone up there, totally vulnerable to fate, betrayed by my own dreams. The need for sleep was wringing my entrails. Something told me I only had a few moments of clarity. I pulled off my turban, wrapped it around me several times and tied it to the pommel. Revealing myself to the sun was a last desperate measure. The white hot star was now threatening to burn out my brain where I sat. I could feet myself going dizzy. I started weaving again. I tried to focus. I tied the reins and laid them on the mare's neck.

"There," I said, "I can do no more than that."

I clicked to Shavon and she began to walk, slowly, as if to tell me she would not throw me off.

I told myself to stay awake but the motion, the unknown illness, the sun, the thirst, the weakness, all conspired to destroy me. Within moments I was unconscious again, slumped in the saddle like a corpse.

From that moment on Shavon was in total command. She could have stopped in her tracks or wandered off in search of grazing. Instead she took me faithfully on a journey through a land of dreams where it was hot and dark. We traveled on and on forever, until somewhere in the distant future I could feel the air growing cooler. The darkness became complete but Shavon kept walking, insisting on taking me to some destination whose importance I couldn't recall. It grew cold in my dreams and utterly black.

Eventually I felt her stop and I heard voices from far away.

I wanted to open my eyes but couldn't, wanted to speak but couldn't find the strength to move my lips.

As unseen hands pulled me down from the saddle I remember hearing, "Shokor Allah (Thank God he is alive)."

And that is all I knew.

Several days later the government doctor told me I had hepatitis. I protested, saying I had to go on to Afghanistan.

"Your liver is shot," he told me. "If you leave here on that horse you'll be dead in two days. I guarantee it."

I protested again. How could he be so sure? Was there a test for the illness? He handed me a dirty test tube, told me to go out back and urinate in it, then bring him the results. I did as I was told.

Minutes later the doctor held the test tube up in front of the window. The morning light revealed a batch of warm urine the color of Coca-Cola. He swished it around, took a quick look, then turned to me and said, "Yep. Hepatitis."

So with that casual comment he brought down the curtain on my horse trip. Shavon was sold to a rug merchant in the Chitral bazaar. My saddle I carried with me when I staggered onto the weekly plane to Peshawar.

As for the Turkoman mujahadeen, the mounted horsemen I had struggled so hard to find, the gallant freedom fighters Shavon had sacrificed to bring me to? They were nowhere to be found!

This is an excerpt from "Khyber Knights" by CuChullaine O'Reilly.

CuChullaine O'Reilly and Shavon.

Chapter 19
Vagabond
by
Jeremy James

One learns that on the equestrian road to adventure a horse and rider share a great many blessings, an unavoidable degree of hardship and a bond so deep it defies common definition. You won't discover it riding in the ring. You won't discover it on a trail ride. You won't discover it in show-jumping, polo, dressage, or western pleasure. You won't discover it until you join that tiny handful of men and women who have suffered in the saddle searching for the answer to an ancient, elusive nomadic longing. Theirs is a secret that can't be bought.

These special few represent the one percent of riders and horses who have roasted in the sun, frozen in the snows, and ultimately achieved a symbiotic emotional relationship unique between the two species.

No one demonstrates this better than the unique Welsh equestrian traveler, Jeremy James. His is an unvarnished love of horses. He speaks to them as if they were smaller siblings. Though other authors reference their mounts in loving literary terms, Jeremy gives them a voice in their mutual story. Plus, he understands and expresses the magic that can only be discovered from the saddle.

"If you travel on a horse you feel the world as you move through it, every step, every scent, every breeze, every dimple in the ground, and it's always fresh."

In 1990 Jeremy set out on a 4,500 kilometre ride from Bulgaria, north to England. He was accompanied by a Gypsy gelding, Sir Karo, and Pusa, a Romanian mare. Travelling through the newly-freed communist countries of Eastern Europe, the happy-go-lucky trio encountered a series of adventures. Yet ultimately Jeremy reached an emotional crossroads that demanded a strict accounting.

I was glad to be alone again, alone with the horses, though I was far from happy about carrying on. My money was low, it was a long way to England and I'd been in the saddle for longer than I had originally anticipated. The journey seemed to have gone flat and I wondered about chucking it in.

Pusa
Do you hear that? Fishface is talking about going home.

Sir Karo
What about us? What will happen to us?
Pusa
Where will we live?
Sir Karo
Who will feed us?
Pusa
Who will look after us?
Sir Karo
What will happen?
Pusa
He's going to sell us!
Sir Karo
He can't! He can't He promised!
Pusa
He promised!

As I was debating what to do, I had the horses shod again, using the same shoes that went on way back in Hungary. The blacksmith had a dry line in observations. There was a girl in the stable when the shoes were going on and she translated. I asked what the blacksmith thought of democracy. He straightened his back and waving a horseshoe at me answered, "Tell me what democracy is and I'll tell you what I think of it."

I asked what would happen to the collectives now Czechoslovakia was supposed to be democratic.

"Ninch!" He said. "Nothing."

"Of Havel? What do you think of Havel?"

"He's a writer."

"And?"

"He's a writer."

I looked out of the cobwebbed window at the rain. I didn't feel like tackling those mountains at all, the very thought of going on was a nightmare: I was fed up with mountains. On the map they looked huge, strung along with a valley full of cranes and lorries. I looked back at the horses. How could I leave them? But how could I take them? I had 650 dollars and reckoned England two to three months' ride at least. At its most generous that was about ten dollars a day and didn't include incidentals like shoeing, fixing visas, the possibility of quarantine or transport across the English Channel, which I knew would be at least 200 pounds, nearly half my money. One way or another, it didn't look as if I was going to make it. Pelham Publishing had already given me more than they agreed to and things looked bleak. Somewhere along the line I was going to have to sell the horses.

But I don't like selling horses. And, besides, there was something else.

You might remember the mountains in Romania, about a night when we were caught out? I said something happened in those mountains and that I'd tell you about it later? Well this is it.

Shortly after Andre left I was up in the mountains with Karo and Pusa and we were caught in rain. We were in thick woodland and night was falling. Under the trees it was wet and the tiny path we'd followed so faithfully had dwindled to nothing beneath our feet; we were confounded, homeless, hungry and soaked. We'd gone too far to turn back and I didn't know how much further that forest went on. I felt pretty scared. You know, those forests in Transylvania are huge and very lonely places.

Night closed around us in a web and darkness sneaked about cold and mean. We were frightened, the three of us. It was a very eerie place and bushes seemed to move the way they do at nightfall, when you're alone. All was silent but for the rain and the wind and murmur of the trees.

And there, in that darkness I held Karo's and Pusa's heads close to mine. I could see their eyes straining, the white at the edges, and steam rising off their flanks even as the darkness deepened and rain hissed in the trees. And as I held their heads close to mine, I felt their breath in my face and felt their fear and uncertainty, and I wanted to end their fear and uncertainty, and made them a promise, and the promise I made was this. I promised them that I would take them to my home. I promised them they wouldn't have to walk anymore, that I would take their shoes off and they could play and graze in the fields that look over the changing colours of the Beacon, where the streams lie, facing south, in the eye of the sun. In winter I would cook them hot barley and put jackets on them at night when it was cold. I promised them they would live in the old stone barn with Gonzo, my Criollo gelding, and Dolly, a dapple-grey Welsh who belongs to my friend and neighbour Alan Watkin. I promised Pusa that when her time came, she could have her foal in the old barn and I would find a name that would be a reflection of her, the journey she made and the land she came from, and I promised Karo that he would never be afraid again. This was the promise I made to my horses that night in Transylvania.

For the rest of that night we stood together in the darkness in silence as the trees tossed their heads and the storm raged about us. Then, as the first hint of dawn struck the night sky as dim as the coat of an iron-grey, I took a reading on my compass from its tiny tritium light and we went down through the trees into a deepening chasm and stones rolled away wet beneath us. We followed that tiny light all the way, weaving through the forest until the sky and trees filled with day and at noon we burst into a green and shining world with flying fields and distant blue hills.

There we stopped. Karo and Pusa grazed for two, three hours and I hung clothes and saddle cloths out to dry, then in the afternoon, we went on.

But the promise was made, and whatever the odds set against us, I steeled myself to honour it.

When the horses were shod in that barn in Czechoslovakia, I saddled them, put the pack on Pusa, left the maps on a wall and we went out into the rain, to Poland.

This is an excerpt from "Vagabond" by Jeremy James.

Jeremy James and Sir Karo.

Chapter 20
Saddlebags for Suitcases
by
Mary Bosanquet

The year 1939 was a bleak and gloomy time in England. Fire and darkness loomed on the horizon as war with Nazi Germany drew ever closer. In the midst of this national angst young Mary Bosanquet had a revelation. She would toss off college in London, board a steam-ship, voyage to Vancouver, Canada, then buy and ride a horse alone more than 2,500 miles to New York City. Simple enough ! She could ride, had a grand total of eighty English pounds to fund the one-woman expedition, and figured horses would be cheap out in the Wild West of Canada. Besides, she reasoned, if the world really was going to self-destruct, she wanted a memorable adventure, "such as befell heroic voyagers," before the global ship sank.

She got one!

Bosanquet rode through the mighty Rockies, was wooed by love-struck cowboys, chased by a grizzly bear, feasted with lonely-trappers, adopted for the winter by a family of Irish farmers, and even suspected of being a Nazi spy, scouting out Canada in preparation for a German invasion. And through it all she had Jonty, her whimsical and charming gelding.

If the two inseparable companions sought to put the news of Europe's descent into madness behind them, by taking refuge in the silent mountains, dreamy forests and mighty plains of pristine Canada, then their eighteen-month trip provided the sanctuary they had longed for. Yet sadly, all equestrian trips must come to a end, and ultimately Mary Bosanquet had to not only return to the barren ugliness that was now war-torn Europe, she was first filled with the sadness of an inevitable parting.

"Last things, last things, how they hurt," she recalled, as she said goodbye to the horse that had changed her life.

So we rode southward all day, and the outlines of hills began to appear. The White Mountains south-east of us, south-west the Adirondacks, and at last between them, fairy-pale, the Green Mountains of Vermont.

Late in the afternoon we reached the border village of Sainte Armande; and that night Jonty and I reached St. Albans, our first town in the United States.

Next day, in dazzling sunshine, we left the little town and began to climb up into the mountains. First the road streamed wide and open over gently sloping grassland, but by midday we were already on rough rocky trails, winding out way among the hills. Just now the Green Mountains are not green; in the pale colours of the dying autumn, silver and copper and old gold, the hill-sides wait for winter. Yesterday was one of those days when one looks and looks, afraid to miss anything; one seizes sudden pictures and says, "I must remember this."

I remember how, as we went up between the wide fields, I looked west and saw a farm-house dark against the vivid sky, with a sculptured line of maples beside it, and behind it the blue Adirondacks running southward beyond Lake Champlain. I remember later another house, very small against a wall of bush, clad in the white smoke from its chimney, and looking like the back-set for an opera. And there was the strange mountain. We came out of the woods, and there it was, all of a sudden among the little rounded hills – a mountain of naked rock cutting into the sky.

When the sunshine was reddening already towards the afternoon, we came down into a valley in which a little lake lay nestling under the shoulders of the hills. The road came winding down out of the trees and crossed the river which fed the lake, upon a white bridge. I stopped on the crest of the bridge to talk to a plain kindly faced woman with a little girl.

"That's a beautiful horse," she said, looking at Jonty, who was shining in the sun.

"There isn't another horse like this one in the world," I replied happily, for what must have been the several hundredth time. "I'm wondering," I added after a little more conversation, "where we shall stay the night."

"Oh, I would think anyone would be tickled to death to have you," replied the little woman.

Her predictions, however, proved to be over-optimistic. At sunset we were wending our way along a small road bordered by comfortable-looking farms. I went to the door of one and asked if we might stay the night. But the lady of the house looked at me forbiddingly from behind the screen-door, and replied that she had not a spare bed. I went on. Four farm-houses turned us down. Feeling small and negligible as a leaf in the wind, I wandered on into the gathering dusk, trailing Jonty behind me and wishing I was either child enough to cry or adult enough not to want to.

At last we reached a farm-house where, after considering us carefully, they took us in. But it is evident that the women of Vermont are more surprised than delighted by the appearance of a solitary girl on a pony.

It seems that the first night did not provide a fair sample of the reception which one may expect to receive in Vermont. For on the next evening I was gladly welcomed into the first house at which I knocked, the only concern of the Polish family who inhabited it being that their spare bedroom was not heated. Soon I was sitting down with them to a huge supper of veal, potatoes, carrots, cream cheese and delicious rye bread; and having done full justice to this repast, I went thankfully to bed.

Next morning I woke to find that it had rained all night, but now the wind was rolling back the curtain of clouds from a back-cloth of blue sky. Jonty and I put down our heads and half closed our eyes and went battling up the road with our tail and rain-coat flapping behind us. We saw little till suddenly I heard a shrill whinny; I looked up, and behold, a dazzling white horse, cantering towards us down the middle of a field, and behind him a bank of grey and copper trees smouldering in shadow, and behind *them* rain and sunshine hunting each other across the mountains. Then I thought of the people who write fairy stories, striving to create something more wonderful than reality, when there could be nothing more wonderful than reality in the mind of anyone on earth.

Meanwhile the horse began to canter along the fence, hooting and jeering, while Jonty ignored him with regal disdain. Jonty has perfect manners with regard to other horses. No matter what demonstrations they make, he goes on unmoved, looking solemnly straight ahead of him, like a good girl who gets winked at in church.

Jonty's extreme virtue on the trip almost worries me sometimes. One of the factors which make a long-distance ride very hard on a horse is the fact that he has so little fun. A healthy horse, like a healthy human being, enjoys physical self-expression. He likes to go prancing out in the morning, play up a little, show off to the other horses, collect himself, play with the bit, use all his paces, per-haps go over a few jumps, and come home, as the writer of Job puts it, still "pawing in the valley and rejoicing in his strength." But on a long-distance trip he cannot do these things. He finds that it does not pay to waste his energy pawing in the valley. He must buckle down to the road and go steadily, from the moment he starts out, if he does not want to be dead tired by evening.

That is why I have always tried to make my longer stays at places where Jonty could have not only rest but recreation. In the West we would stay at ranches, and I would give him runs after cattle. Now I try to find places where there are other horses, and where he can have pleasant and varied exercise in company. I do not stop for long, unless there is a good field. Even in the depths of winter when the grass is covered, it does a horse good to run out, to roll, buck round and feel for a little while that he is a free horse, and nobody in the world can gallop faster than he.

Thanks to the fact that he has never gone very long without relaxation, and thanks to the great heart which is packed into his neat little body, Jonty's temperament has not suffered from the ride. He is as solemn as a judge on the trail, but after a couple of day's rest, he begins rejoicing in his strength again to such an extent that I have both hands full to ride him. So I know that I really need not worry.

We have now passed through Vermont, Massachusetts and into Connecticut, and now I am sitting in bed in a white house on a hill-side, watching the dawn coming over the Berkshire Hills.

In a few days now we shall be in New York, and the ride will be finished. Watching the mists lying white in the valley, I have been sliding my mind back and realizing how many of the unhurried impressions of the last eighteen months will go with me into the years, helping to create day by day the person who is me. Wherever I go from here these things will go after me. Always in my mind there will be mountains running down to the Pacific, great trees and tiny trails and deer, and packers lighting fires and pitching tents and hauling up the slack on a diamond hitch; there will be year-old snow and black tea out of billy-cans and rain in the mountains; but no rain on the scorching range of the dry belt, only cactus and sage-brush and sunflowers burning down the hill-sides.

Rain and sun in the foot-hills though, rivers and ranches, great fantastic Western saddles on little lean broncos, steers bucking to heaven at stampedes, ten-gallon hats and high-heeled boots and close-fitting overalls on bandy legs, horses milling in high corrals and little ranch houses filling with unexpected guests. After that, sunsets over the wheat fields and northern lights arching up into the sky, and straight sandy roads which go on almost forever, and grain elevators and cottonwood trees and the rare delight of river-valleys.

Then Winnipeg, and the wilderness beyond, and tamaracks burning gold out on the blue-black swamps, naked rocks and lonely lakes shivering in the wind. Then the vast expanse of Lake Superior, and the winter spent in the warm safety of the Skerten family farm – lamplight in the early morning kitchen – milking time in misty barns – teams labouring out of the bush – spring and syrup-boiling under budding maples, daisied hay standing high, and a boat floating down a river on the trail of a timber drive.

Autumn again under the shoulder of Laurentians, and so at last this gold and silver journey through the Green Mountains of Vermont. And always, through everything, the horse with me, tireless and kind, giving me his unchanging companionship, his unbroken trust. Remembering Canada, I remember too the majesty of Vancouver, standing between the mountains and the sea, Calgary and Winnipeg on the borders of the prairies, Ottawa with the Parliament Houses standing upon their hill, and Montreal grouped round its royal mountain.

But when the seas divide me from her, Canada will live for me, not in the memory of her cities, but of hip-roofed barns and snake fences and stout corrals, of the dark flash of a red-winged blackbird and the snort of little branded bronco, of mountains and wheat fields and the wilderness. For the soul of Canada is not in her cities. And I do not believe that the soul of the world is in cities either, or ever can be.

All these last days, following large scale maps, Jonty and I have been wandering down the by-ways of Connecticut. Tomorrow our journey together will be over.

It is terrible to love horses like this, to love one horse like this, and to have to part with him. Often in these last days I get down and walk, because then Jonty follows along with his head close to my shoulder, and so I seem to be nearer to him. Whatever people say, a horse does not often become deeply attached to a person. But this has happened to Jonty. To part with a horse who will not miss one is bad, but to part with a horse who will miss one is as bad as anything I know.

Sometimes I put my round his neck and fit my face into the hollow behind his cheek. But this surprises and annoys him, and he shakes his head impatiently. So there is nothing to do but walk beside him, as I have walked so many times before.

So we have made it. Encouraged by an escort of mounted police, little Jonty carried me in undaunted – through Harlem, through the Bronx, down the narrow length of Central Park, down Eighth Avenue and into the Mounted Police Barracks on Forty-eighth Street, where he is temporarily installed.

It is evening now, and I sit to write at the window of my cousin's thirteenth floor flat. Far below goes by the muted roar of the traffic upon Park Avenue. Before me the lighted windows of the sky-scrapers tower into the dark.

So ends the journal of an experiment in adventure !

This is an excerpt from "Saddlebags for Suitcases" by Mary Bosanquet, published by The Long Riders' Guild Press.

Mary Bosanquet and Jonty

Epilogue
Equestrian Argonauts –
The Story of The Long Riders' Guild
by
Darcy Morger-Grovenstein

They are the superlatives of horseback riding. They move through extremes, unknown to most of us, even in our dreams. Consummate adventurers, they are saddle veterans of at least one requisite 1000-mile horse trek. This special brand of riders does not ride for a laurelled crown, won by speed or mileage charts, any more than they do a buckle for a spin around an arena. They ride for the sheer joy of freedom felt upon a horse. When the fast-paced modern world threatens to encroach upon such lives, they ride out to immerse themselves in the elements of earth. They extend an excitement to other souls aching to do the same by saying, "You can do this too! Mount up and come away!" They are ardent seekers of the trail. A growing breed of equestrians with traditions and ancestors as old as history itself, they are called, "The Long Riders."

Travelers in a world set apart.

Until a few years ago, these exotic equestrian travelers had to find and ride the road solo. Those making such arduous journeys were disconnected from others on similar quests. Knowledge of such undertakings was limited to a smattering of out-of-print books and faint tales of saddle pilgrims. Some had made it and some had not. All had made mistakes. Yet a common body of knowledge for those wishing to make such journeys did not exist. In fact, by the middle of the 20th Century, the domain of nomadic travel was almost completely lost.

Then, in the mid-1990s, one CuChullaine O'Reilly, Long Rider and visionary entered the picture. Just back in the States after traversing the breadth of Pakistan and aching for fellowship with similar souls, O'Reilly was immersed in writing a book about his experiences crossing Pakistan. He happened upon two such Americans who had likewise completed a 10,000 mile journey from the Atlantic to the Pacific coasts. Tracy Paine and DC Vision affirmed O'Reilly's yearning to find and unite such horsemen and women. They discussed the invention of such an association.

Now enter one lady of interest – Basha Gypsy Moon, vanguard as well, an Anglo-Swiss woman and veteran of a Long Ride in 1995 from Stalingrad, Russia to England. In fact, the only person to ride out of Russia in the 20th Century. Equally passionate about equestrian travel and ardent in uniting such riders, Basha and CuChullaine met and discovered in each other their soul mate. They married in 2001, and have not been apart one day since.

This pair, along with American DC Vision and Canadian Danny Candella, laid the groundwork for the first international meeting of Long Riders. DC believed creating this organization as a "Guild" would give an historic sense to its identity. All four co-founders agreed. The Long Riders' Guild was born.

The new guild was formed in the year 2000, at the dawn of a new millennium, and would be a haven of comradeship for all those who had earned the distinction of "Long Rider." The Guild would preserve stories and precious knowledge passed down from 6000 years of horse travel. It would research and acknowledge the unlauded victors of past adventures. It would promote continued equestrian exploration, and excursions of the future. The Long Riders' Guild would become an international alliance committed to the values of 'equestrian knighthood' – honesty, compassion, loyalty, honor, courtesy, spirituality, and courage.

Long Riders know that the true importance of a quest is not the destination but what happens in the process of getting there. It is this process that becomes the impetus for a life-changing experience. All too cognizant of what a thousand miles will do to one's soul in the saddle, they want others who are sincerely interested to share in the same. They value each and every person's right to "go the distance."

The first four Founding Members of The Long Riders' Guild, from three different countries, intentionally created it as non-exclusionary. The Long Riders are, in fact, defined by their diversity with only the mutual love of horse and travel in their midst. Just in its third official year, The Guild's membership and The Historical Long Riders' rosters are an eclectic blend of past and present humankind. No particular profession or status in life is the predication of a Long Rider. Listed among them are poets, scientists, explorers, monarchs, scholars, musicians, writers, lumberjacks, actresses, noblemen and noblewomen, and even 7 and 11-year-old brothers, and all that is and was between. They are people who have moved from the ordinary to the extraordinary by the mastery of such miles beneath the hooves of their mounts. Today's 200+ Long Riders are from 31 countries and all six inhabited continents. The Guild library contains books contributed by members with manuscripts in fifteen different languages. The statistics covering these members is incredible. It covers every sort of age and physical boundary imaginable.

There are a few exceptions, however, to The Guild's "open door" policy. The Long Riders' Guild is not interested in accepting for membership those individuals who ride the qualifying 1000 miles at the conscious expense of their horses. Cruelty or the subjection of one's mount to needless suffering is unacceptable. There is no room within the organization of The Long Riders' Guild for those who ride for the purpose of publicity or business for the sake of business. That said, one gets the message that this organization is all about realness, balance, and self-challenge.

In keeping with the non-competitive and inclusive nature of The Guild, two special horse-loving realms have been added to The Long Riders' Guild. One is the "disabled riding programs" and the complement of "carriage" riding.

Long Rider Eleanor Carton Black, who, despite being deaf since birth, rode alone across the United States, has been named as the liaison representative between The Guild and "disabled" riding programs around the world. The Long Riders' Guild website also supports the US Driving for the Disabled program, and has information concerning a carriage journey which was made by Michael Muir and Cindy Goff of the "Driving for the Disabled" organization. Michael has Multiple Sclerosis (MS) and Cindy is confined to a wheelchair. The pair, who made a 1000-mile trip from Louisville, Kentucky to Florida, drove a specially built carriage. What makes this ride even more special is that the route followed in the footsteps of Michael's great-grandfather, John Muir, famed naturalist and founder of the Sierra Club.

In an unprecedented move, the prestigious Royal Geographical Society (RGS) of England decided in November 2002 to induct all members of The Long Riders' Guild as Fellows. The RGS made this decision due to the courage and outstanding achievements of individual Long Riders as well as the academic contributions of The Long Riders' Guild to the world of geographic exploration.

The Long Riders' Guild has gone where no man has gone before, literally and electronically speaking. It is a blend of the ageless passion the rider has for his horse and the magic of the modern age of Internet. It is probably the first of its kind where Guild members find each other not within the four walls of a castle but via a website. Housing more than 1000 pages, The Guild's website accepts no advertisements, and is committed to its goals of preserving equestrian history and encouraging equestrian travel. The Long Riders' Guild website provides this information free of charge to the reader on a myriad of topics from equine history and updates on current expeditions to equestrian travel guidance and tack room tips.

Founders Basha and CuChullaine O'Reilly don't just spout words and epitaphs to riders from an electronic page, they live the dream every day. Currently the two are planning their next "Long Ride" – the first non-stop, around-the-world equestrian journey! CuChullaine defines the character of a Long Rider as this:

No one can define a journey for us.
No one is privy to what frightens us.
No one can toss us into the air and make us fly.
It is only when we discover the courage in our own hearts that we can find the strength to put our foot in that stirrup.
Take a deep breath and push off from gravity – from the predictable lives we have led,
From those who tell us it can't be done.
From the village that has restricted us.
From all the life-threatening things that sap our souls and steal our bravery.
Being a Long Rider is:
About having MS and making the journey of a lifetime anyway;
About being five years old and not knowing you're doing something "impossible."
About being 69 years old and doing something "impossible" AGAIN.
About being one of the few.

So tonight when you retire to a bed you know and easy comfort, just let your dreams fly one more time. Toss them up high into the air and see how they would look with you actually living them. And now you know that there are others, throughout all of history, who have done the same and followed through. They have become the ones who would help you, whatever your quest may be. For they have gone ahead before, they saw their dreams and grabbed them, held them fast, then to took to flight on the back of a steed.

Make a vow to yourself not to let one more day pass. Take on the journeys you thought were only for someone else. Become that Long Rider who already lives within your soul!

LONG RIDERS OF SPECIAL RECOGNITION:
Gene Glasscock: Gene has already ridden from the Arctic Circle to the Equator. Now he is on a 20,000 mile trek to the 48 continental state capitols. Gene was the guest of honor at the national BLM ceremony in Washington, DC, on October 11th, 2003 – Gene's 69th birthday!

Otto Schwarz, of Switzerland, has more travel miles in the saddle than anyone alive today. The 83-year-old has traveled more than 35,000 miles in the saddle and has ridden on every continent except Antarctica.

Fawn Fields, the youngest living Long Rider, at the age of five rode 1200 miles from Carlton, Texas to Prescott, Arizona alongside the horse-drawn wagon driven by her parents.

Ginny Shumaker, an American woman who rode from Ohio to Los Angeles in the summer of 1941, then after the Japanese bombed Pearl Harbor, Ginny rode from Ohio to New York where she led a contingency of Hollywood movie stars, including Gene Autry, down a Fifth Avenue Ticker-Tape Parade. The parade kicked off the country's first war bond drive. Ginny is 83 years old.

George Patterson of Scotland rode across the Himalayas from Tibet to India during the winter of 1949 in order to tell the outside world that the Communist Chinese were invading Tibet. George is also 83.

Jose Hernandez of Mexico, though legally blind, rode all the way from San Diego, California, to Washington, DC.

Kareen Kohn, a famous Israeli Long Rider, recently completed a horse trek from Ecuador to the Incan ruins in Peru. This is how he poetically defined a "Long Rider:"

"The new nomad is born.
With the passion of the Gypsy.
The tolerance of the Bedouin.
The flare of the Artist.
The courage of the Warrior.
The instinct of the Indian.
The madness of a Prophet
And the hope of a Dreamer."

This article, originally entitled "The Long Riders: "Equestrian Argonauts of the Dream," first appeared in the January, 2004 issue of "Trail Blazer" magazine. It appears in this anthology courtesy of the author, Darcy Morger-Grovenstein and Trail Blazer's publisher, Susan Gibson.

Coming in Volume Two of The Long Riders Anthology

The greatest collection of mounted adventure stories continues to canter towards you. Volume Two will contain twenty more equestrian episodes including :

"To Save a Country"
The Khamba warlord in Tibet had given George Patterson a deadly mission - carry word to the outside world that the Chinese Communists were about to secretly invade the mountain kingdom. The problem was that the winter of 1949 had turned the mighty Himalayas into a wall of ice and the only trail leading to India had never been traveled by horsemen! Could the young Scot mounted on a Tibetan horse survive the snow covered journey and bring back help to his adopted homeland?

"Spanish Pilgrimage"
Robin Hanbury Tenison has led a life filled with adventure, starting in 1958 when he made the first crossing of South America at its widest point. The Royal Geographical Society awarded him a Gold Medal for his various explorations in other far-flung corners of the world. Then he turned his hand to equestrian travel, thereafter writing four of the most charming horse travel tales of modern times. Robin was accompanied by his wife, Louella, as they made their romantic rides, including their journey across the Iberian Peninsula. This delightful tale recalls how Robin and Louella make their way over a thousand-year-old pilgrim's path towards the mythical Santiago de Compostela, the sacred cathedral of Spain.

"By Desert Ways to Baghdad and Damascus"
Louisa Jebb had a private mission, to saddle up her horse in 1900 and ride off in search of adventure across the desert regions of the fading Ottoman Empire. Louisa couldn't speak the local languages. Nor had any other foreign lady travelers ever attempted such a mounted feat before. But not to be dissuaded, Louise set out from Constantinople accompanied by female cousin and a saddlebag full of courage and optimism. What befell the two young English ladies was nothing less than mounted magic as they were invited into forbidden harems, dined as the daughters of pashas, and took a last glimpse at an Oriental world now swept away by the fortunes of many wars.

"Mi Amigo, Don Roberto"
In 1925 Aimé Tschiffely, a Swiss teacher living in Argentina, set out on the most epic ride of the 20th century. The amateur explorer's goal was to travel ten thousand miles from Buenos Aires to Washington, DC, over some of the world's most inhospitable country, with his two Criollo horses, Mancha and Gato. Their odyssey lasted two and a half years, forced horses and rider to survive through

near-impossible conditions, and ended with a hero's welcome at the White House. What few people know is that the most famous equestrian travel story of all time was very nearly never told. The Long Rider manuscript that changed history was rescued from obscurity by another famous equestrian explorer, the Scotsman turned gaucho known as Don Roberto Cunninghame-Graham. Revealed here for the first time, and incorporating never before published family documents and photos from Tschiffely and Don Roberto's literary heir, read about the astonishing ride, and the amazing friendship, that changed the course of modern equestrian travel history forever

"Ride the Wind"

Once they were famous from the Atlantic to the Pacific. Every school child knew their names. And why not? Bud and Temple Abernathy had made history more than once. In 1909 the small brothers, aged nine and five, rode more than 1,000 miles from Oklahoma Territory to Santa Fe, New Mexico and back – ALONE ! The following year the intrepid youngsters set their sights on New York city, and rode 1,400 miles there to meet Teddy Roosevelt. Once again, they had made their ride without any adult assistance. Then in 1911 the tiny Long Riders set out to do the impossible – and they did. They rode nearly 4,000 miles from New York to San Francisco in 62 days, thereby accomplishing a historic ride, without any adult assistance, which has never been equaled. Relive and relearn the forgotten story of the most amazing Long Riders who ever cantered into history.

Coming in Spring, 2005

OUR CURRENT LIST OF TITLES

Abernathy, Miles, *Ride the Wind* – the amazing true story of the little Abernathy Boys, who made a series of astonishing journeys in the United States, starting in 1909 when they were aged five and nine!

Beard, John, *Saddles East* – John Beard determined as a child that he wanted to see the Wild West from the back of a horse after a visit to Cody's legendary Wild West show. Yet it was only in 1948 – more than sixty years after seeing the flamboyant American showman – that Beard and his wife Lulu finally set off to follow their dreams.

Beker, Ana, *The Courage to Ride* – Determined to out-do Tschiffely, Beker made a 17,000 mile mounted odyssey across the Americas in the late 1940s that would fix her place in the annals of equestrian travel history.

Bird, Isabella, *Among the Tibetans* – A rousing adventure, an enchanting travelogue, a forgotten peek at a mountain kingdom swept away by the waves of time.

Bird, Isabella, *A Lady's Life in the Rocky Mountains* – The story of Isabella Bird's adventures during the winter of 1873 when she explored the magnificent unspoiled wilderness of Colorado. Truly a classic.

Bosanquet, Mary, *Saddlebags for Suitcases* – In 1939 Bosanquet set out to ride from Vancouver, Canada, to New York. Along the way she was wooed by love-struck cowboys, chased by a grizzly bear and even suspected of being a Nazi spy, scouting out Canada in preparation for a German invasion. A truly delightful book.

de Bourboulon, Catherine, *Shanghai à Moscou (French)* – the story of how a young Scottish woman and her aristocratic French husband travelled overland from Shanghai to Moscow in the late 19th Century.

Brown, Donald; *Journey from the Arctic* – A truly remarkable account of how Brown, his Danish companion and their two trusty horses attempt the impossible, to cross the silent Arctic plateaus, thread their way through the giant Swedish forests, and finally discover a passage around the treacherous Norwegian marshes.

Burnaby, Frederick; *A Ride to Khiva* – Burnaby fills every page with a memorable cast of characters, including hard-riding Cossacks, nomadic Tartars, vodka-guzzling sleigh-drivers and a legion of peasant ruffians.

Burnaby, Frederick, *On Horseback through Asia Minor* – Armed with a rifle, a small stock of medicines, and a single faithful servant, the equestrian traveler rode through a hotbed of intrigue and high adventure in wild inhospitable country, encountering Kurds, Circassians, Armenians, and Persian pashas.

Carter, General William, *Horses, Saddles and Bridles* – This book covers a wide range of topics including basic training of the horse and care of its equipment. It also provides a fascinating look back into equestrian travel history.

Chase, J. Smeaton, *California Coast Trails* – This classic book describes the author's journey from Mexico to Oregon along the coast of California in the 1890s. Smeaton Chase treats us to a treasure trove of observations, commenting on subjects as diverse as the architecture of the Spanish Missions, the hospitality of the people, and the beauties of a fabled countryside.

Chase, J. Smeaton, *California Desert Trails* – In 1910 the British naturalist made his second mounted exploration, this time wending his way through the Mojave Desert of California. The resultant book is amply illustrated with stunning black and white photographs and includes a special appendix wherein Chase gives "Hints on Desert Traveling."

Clark, Leonard, *The Marching Wind* – The panoramic story of a mounted exploration in the remote and savage heart of Asia, a place where adventure, danger, and intrigue were the daily backdrop to wild tribesman and equestrian exploits.

Cobbett, William, *Rural Rides, Volumes 1 and 2* – In the early 1820s Cobbett set out on horseback to make a series of personal tours through the English countryside. These books contain what many believe to be the best accounts of rural England ever written, and remain enduring classics.

Codman, John, *Winter Sketches from the Saddle* – This classic book was first published in 1888. It recommends riding for your health and describes the septuagenarian author's many equestrian journeys through New England during the winter of 1887 on his faithful mare, Fanny.

Daly, H.W., *Manual of Pack Transportation* – This book is the author's masterpiece. It contains a wealth of information on various pack saddles, ropes and equipment, how to secure every type of load imaginable and instructions on how to organize a pack train.

Dixie, Lady Florence, *Riding Across Patagonia* – When asked in 1879 why she wanted to travel to such an outlandish place as Patagonia, the author replied without hesitation that she was taking to the saddle in order to flee from the strict confines of polite Victorian society. This is the story of how the aristocrat successfully traded the perils of a London parlor for the wind-borne freedom of a wild Patagonian bronco.

Farson, Negley, *Caucasian Journey* – A thrilling account of a dangerous equestrian journey made in 1929, this is an amply illustrated adventure classic.

Fox, Ernest, *Travels in Afghanistan* – The thrilling tale of a 1937 journey through the mountains, valleys, and deserts of this forbidden realm, including visits to such fabled places as the medieval city of Heart, the towering Hindu Kush mountains, and the legendary Khyber Pass.

Galton, Francis, *The Art of Travel* – Originally published in 1855, this book became an instant classic and was used by a host of now-famous explorers, including Sir Richard Francis Burton of Mecca fame. Readers can learn how to ride horses, handle elephants, avoid cobras, pull teeth, find water in a desert, and construct a sleeping bag out of fur.

Glazier, Willard, *Ocean to Ocean on Horseback* – This book about the author's journey from New York to the Pacific in 1875 contains every kind of mounted adventure imaginable. Amply illustrated with pen and ink drawings of the time, the book remains a timeless equestrian adventure classic.

Goodwin, Joseph, *Through Mexico on Horseback* – The author and his companion, Robert Horiguichi, the sophisticated, multi-lingual son of an imperial Japanese diplomat, set out in 1931 to cross Mexico. They were totally unprepared for the deserts, quicksand and brigands they were to encounter during their adventure.

Hanbury-Tenison, Robin, *White Horses over France* – The story of a magical journey made by the famous British explorer, Robin Hanbury Tenison, and his wife Louella, as they set off in 1984 to ride Camargue horses from the south of France to their faraway farm in Cornwall, England.

Hanbury-Tenison, Robin, *Chinese Adventure* – The Hanbury Tenisons take to the saddle again, deciding in 1986 to ride 1,000 miles alongside the Great Wall of China. What occurs is a magnificent mounted journey through a remarkable country.

Hanbury-Tenison, Robin, *Fragile Eden* – This time the Hanbury Tenisons are off to picturesque New Zealand in 1988, searching for adventure as they ride through some of the most dramatic high-country in the world.

Hanbury-Tenison, Robin, *Spanish Pilgrimage* – With countless miles under their saddles, Robin and Louella Hanbury Tenison set off on their last journey, a romantic ride across Spain, which culminates with their arrival at the ancient cathedral of Santiago de Compostela.

Haslund, Henning, *Mongolian Adventure* – An epic tale inhabited by a cast of characters no longer present in this lackluster world, shamans who set themselves on fire, rebel leaders who sacked towns, and wild horsemen whose ancestors conquered the world.

Heath, Frank, *Forty Million Hoofbeats* – Heath set out in 1925 to follow his dream of riding to all 48 of the Continental United States. The journey lasted more than two years, during which time Heath and his mare, Gypsy Queen, became inseparable companions.

Holt, William, *Ride a White Horse* – After rescuing a cart horse, Trigger, from slaughter and nursing him back to health, the 67-year-old Holt and his horse set out in 1964 on an incredible 9,000 mile, non-stop journey through western Europe.

Hopkins, Frank T., *Hidalgo and Other Stories* – For the first time in history, here are the collected writings of Frank T. Hopkins, the counterfeit cowboy whose endurance racing claims and Old West fantasies have polarized the equestrian world.

James, Jeremy, *Saddletramp* – The classic story of Jeremy James' journey from Turkey to Wales, on an unplanned route with an inaccurate compass, unreadable map and the unfailing aid of villagers who seemed to have as little sense of direction as he had.

James, Jeremy, *Vagabond* – The wonderful tale of the author's journey from Bulgaria to Berlin offers a refreshing, witty and often surprising view of Eastern Europe and the collapse of communism.

Jebb, Louisa, *By Desert Ways to Baghdad and Damascus* – Two young English women set off in 1900 to explore the desert regions of the fading Ottoman Empire. What they encounter was nothing short of mounted magic as they are invited into forbidden harems, dined as daughters of pashas and take in a last glimpse of an Oriental world now swept away by the fortunes of war.

Kluckhohn, Clyde, *To the Foot of the Rainbow* – This is not just a exciting true tale of equestrian adventure. It is a moving account of a young man's search for physical perfection in a desert world still untouched by the recently-born twentieth century.

Lambie, Thomas, *Boots and Saddles in Africa* – Lambie's story of his equestrian journeys is told with the grit and realism that marks a true classic.

Landor, Henry Savage, *In the Forbidden Land* – Illustrated with hundreds of photographs and drawings, this blood-chilling account of equestrian adventure makes for page-turning excitement.

Leigh, Margaret, *My Kingdom for a Horse* – In the autumn of 1939 the author rode from Cornwall to Scotland, resulting in one of the most delightful equestrian journeys of the early twentieth century. This book is full of keen observations of a rural England that no longer exists.

Maillart, Ella, *Turkestan Solo* – A vivid account of a 1930s journey through this wonderful, mysterious and dangerous portion of the world, complete with its Kirghiz eagle hunters, lurking Soviet secret police, and the timeless nomads that still inhabited the desolate steppes of Central Asia.

MacCann, William *(Spanish)*, *Viaje a Caballo* – Amateur scientist, turned equestrian explorer, William MacCann set out to explore Argentina by horse in

1848. What followed was a unique narrative packed with cultural observations and pampas horse tradition.

Marcy, Randolph, *The Prairie Traveler* – There were a lot of things you packed into your saddlebags or the wagon before setting off to cross the North American wilderness in the 1850s. A gun and an axe were obvious necessities. Yet many pioneers were just as adamant about placing a copy of Captain Randolph Marcy's classic book close at hand.

Muir Watson, Sharon, *The Colour of Courage* – The remarkable true story of the epic horse trip made by the first people to travel Australia's then-unmarked Bicentennial National Trail. There are enough adventures here to satisfy even the most jaded reader.

O'Reilly, CuChullaine, *Khyber Knights* – Told with grit and realism by one of the world's foremost equestrian explorers, "Khyber Knights" has been penned the way lives are lived, not how books are written.

O'Reilly, CuChullaine (editor), *The Long Riders, Volume 1* – An amazing new series begins with twenty of the most famous equestrian travel stories ever told. Here are the mounted mystics seeking inner enlightenment via that altar of travel, the saddle. Here are the daring ones who ride hell-bent for leather through a host of adventures. They ride together for the first time in this illustrated volume dedicated to sharing the mounted adventures of the world's most important Long Riders.

Östrup, J., *Växlande Horisont* – (Swedish) – The thrilling tale of a young Swedish student who travels across Asia Minor in 1891 on his Arab stallion in search of adventure.

Pocock, Roger, *Following the Frontier* – Pocock was one of the nineteenth century's most influential equestrian travelers. Within the covers of this book is the detailed account of Pocock's horse ride along the infamous Outlaw Trail, a 3,000 mile solo journey that took the adventurer from Canada to Mexico City.

Pocock, Roger, *Horses* – Though Pocock enjoyed a reputation for dangerous living, his observations on horses were praised by the leading thinkers of his day. Here is a lost masterpiece of equestrian study, penned by one of the most unique men to ever mount a horse or lift a pen.

Post, Charles Johnson, *Horse Packing* – Originally published in 1914, this book was an instant success, incorporating as it did the very essence of the science of packing horses and mules. It makes fascinating reading for students of the horse or history.

Ray, G. W., *Through Five Republics on Horseback* – In 1889 a British explorer - part-time missionary and full-time adventure junky – set out to find a lost tribe of sun-worshipping natives in the unexplored forests of Paraguay. The journey was so brutal that it defies belief.

Ross, Julian, *Travels in an Unknown Country* – A delightful book about modern horseback travel in the Transylvania mountains of Romania, an enchanting country which once marked the eastern borders of the Roman Empire.

Ross, Martin and Somerville, E.O., *Beggars on Horseback* – Incredibly famous in their day, the aristocratic Irish authors set off in 1894 on a fun-filled equestrian journey across Wales. The result was an enchantingly funny classic of mounted mirth.

Ruxton, George, *Adventures in Mexico* – The story of a young British army officer who rode from Vera Cruz to Santa Fe, Mexico in 1847. At times the author exhibits a fearlessness which borders on insanity. He ignores dire warnings, rides through deadly deserts, and dares murderers to attack him. It is a delightful and invigorating tale of a time and place now long gone.

Schwarz, Hans *(German)*, *Vier Pferde, Ein Hund und Drei Soldaten* – In the early 1930s the author and his two companions rode through Liechtenstein, Austria, Romania, Albania, Yugoslavia, to Turkey, then rode back again! This book is more than just a well-written adventure tale. Schwarz's trip, and the resulting book, inspired three generations of German-speaking Long Riders to take to the saddle.

Schwarz, Otto *(German), Reisen mit dem Pferd* – the Swiss Long Rider with more miles in the saddle than anyone else tells his wonderful story, and a long appendix tells the reader how to follow in his footsteps.

Scott, Robert, *Scott's Last Expedition* – Many people are unaware that Scott recruited Siberian ponies for his doomed expedition to the South Pole in 1909. Here is the remarkable story of men and horses who all paid the ultimate sacrifice.

Skrede, Wilfred, *Across the Roof of the World* – This epic equestrian travel tale of a wartime journey across Russia, China, Turkestan and India is laced with unforgettable excitement.

Stevens, Thomas, *Through Russia on a Mustang* – Mounted on his faithful horse, Texas, Stevens crossed the Steppes in search of adventure. Cantering across the pages of this classic tale is a cast of nineteenth century Russian misfits, peasants, aristocrats—and even famed Cossack Long Rider Dmitri Peshkov.

Stevenson, Robert L., *Travels with a Donkey* – In 1878, the author set out to explore the remote Cevennes mountains of France. He travelled alone, unless you count his stubborn and manipulative pack-donkey, Modestine. This book is a true classic.

Strong, Anna Louise, *Road to the Grey Pamir* – With Stalin's encouragement, Strong rode into the seldom-seen Pamir mountains of faraway Tadjikistan. The political renegade turned equestrian explorer soon discovered more adventure than she had anticipated.

Sykes, Ella, *Through Persia on a Sidesaddle* – Ella Sykes rode side-saddle 2,000 miles across Persia, a country few European woman had ever visited. Mind you, she traveled in style, accompanied by her Swiss maid and 50 camels loaded with china, crystal, linens and fine wine.

Trinkler, Emile, *Through the Heart of Afghanistan* – In the early 1920s the author made a legendary trip across a country now recalled only in legends.

Tschiffely, Aimé, *Bohemia Junction* – "Forty years of adventurous living condensed into one book."

Tschiffely, Aimé, *Bridle Paths* – a final poetic look at a now-vanished Britain.

Tschiffely, Aimé, *The Tale of Two Horses* – The story of Tschiffely's famous journey from Buenos Aires to Washington, DC, narrated by his two equine heroes, Mancha and Gato. Their unique point of view is guaranteed to delight children and adults alike.

Tschiffely, Aimé, *This Way Southward* – the most famous equestrian explorer of the twentieth century decides to make a perilous journey across the U-boat infested Atlantic.

Tschiffely, Aimé, *Tschiffely's Ride* – The true story of the most famous equestrian journey of the twentieth century – 10,000 miles with two Criollo geldings from Argentina to Washington, DC. A new edition is coming soon with a Foreword by his literary heir!

Warner, Charles Dudley, *On Horseback in Virginia* – A prolific author, and a great friend of Mark Twain, Warner made witty and perceptive contributions to the world of nineteenth century American literature. This book about the author's equestrian adventures is full of fascinating descriptions of nineteenth century America.

Weale, Magdalene, *Through the Highlands of Shropshire* – It was 1933 and Magdalene Weale was faced with a dilemma: how to best explore her beloved English countryside? By horse, of course! This enchanting book invokes a gentle, softer world inhabited by gracious country lairds, wise farmers, and jolly inn keepers.

Wentworth Day, J., *Wartime Ride* – In 1939 the author decided the time was right for an extended horseback ride through England! While parts of his country were being ravaged by war, Wentworth Day discovered an inland oasis of mellow harvest fields, moated Tudor farmhouses, peaceful country halls, and fishing villages.

Wilkins, Messanie, *Last of the Saddle Tramps* – Told she had little time left to live, the author decided to ride from her native Maine to the Pacific. Accompanied by her faithful horse, Tarzan, Wilkins suffered through any number of obstacles, including blistering deserts and freezing snow storms – and defied the doctors by living for another 20 years!.

de Windt, Harry, *A Ride to India* – Fellow of the Royal Geographical Society and gentleman equestrian explorer par excellence, "Handsome" Harry de Windt decided to ride across Persia in the winter of 1890. He faced a host of inconveniences, including a winter storm which froze his cigar to his lips. But nothing could stop the hero of the Victorian age from riding to his appointed goal, faraway India.

Wilson, Andrew, *The Abode of Snow* – One of the best accounts of overland equestrian travel ever written about the wild lands that lie between Tibet and Afghanistan.

Winthrop, Theodore, *Saddle and Canoe* – This book paints a vibrant picture of 1850s life in the Pacific Northwest and covers the author's travels along the Straits of Juan De Fuca, on Vancouver Island, across the Naches Pass, and on to The Dalles, in Oregon Territory. This is truly an historic travel account.

Younghusband, George, *Eighteen Hundred Miles on a Burmese Pony* – In early 1887 an adventurous young British officer sets off to explore the wilds of back country Burma. Little does he realize that he is about to mount up on the most unlikely horse hero of the age. Complete with pencil drawings done by the author, this delightful book takes the reader on a mounted journey complete with the requisite adventures, but with the added delight of a pint-sized pony you'll never forget.

Our list of titles is constantly being updated, so please check our website, **horsetravelbooks.com** for the latest information.